Summerfest

Cooler by the lake: 40 years of music and memories

Written by Dave Tianen

Edited by Tina Maples

Photographs by
The Milwaukee Journal Sentinel
Milwaukee World Festival Inc.

THE MILWAUKEE JOURNAL SENTINEL

Photography editor: John Klein
Art director: Lonnie Turner
Designer: Carolyn Ryan
Copy editor: William J. Dowlding
Digital technician: Jack Emmrich

Acknowledgements

Research assistance

Milwaukee Journal Sentinel staff: Sarah D. Johnson, Ruth E. Ward, News Information Center. Also: Liz Challice, Joanne Kempinger Demski, Roberta J. Wahlers, Kelly Megna, Marcia Szalewski

Milwaukee World Festival Inc.: Kristin Chuckel, marketing and public relations coordinator, Summerfest; Bob Babisch, entertainment director, Summerfest

Journal Sentinel photographers

Kevin Eisenhut, Mark Hoffman, Joe Koshollek, William J. Lizdas, Tom Lynn, William Meyer, Jack Orton, Jeffrey Phelps, Gary Porter, Michael Sears, Karen Sherlock, Benny Sieu, MaryJo Walicki, Kristyna Wentz-Graff, Rick Wood

Sherman Williams, Assistant Managing Editor/Photography

Berford Gammon III, Director of Photography

Janine Ghelfi, editorial assistant

Dave Kirner, photo technician

Angela Peterson, picture editor

Digital technicians

Jackie Brown, Mark Graham, Dave Leshok

Music review excerpts, from Journal Sentinel archives: Duane Dudek, Jim Higgins, Jackie Loohauis, Tina Maples, Dave Tianen

This book is available in quantity at special discounts for your group or organization. For further information, contact Triumph Books, 542 S. Dearborn St., Suite 750, Chicago, IL 60605. (312) 939-3330. Fax (312) 663-3557

Printed in USA
ISBN: 978-1-60078-049-3

table of
contents

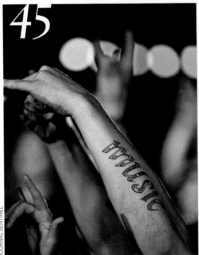

opening act

I didn't go to the first Summerfest, or the second. But I did go to the third.

I remember standing in a dark, muddy field in the rain to see comedian Pat Paulsen in 1970. This was just two years after Paulsen had "run" for president for the first time, and he was a regular on the Smothers Brothers' hit TV show.

Paulsen was one of the hottest comics in the country — and on that night, he was also one of the dampest. The stage, really just a platform, was uncovered, and he got soaked right along with the crowd.

Standing in the middle of that field, there wasn't the slightest glimmer of what Summerfest would become.

In the decades since, 15 weedy acres have become a meticulously groomed, 76-acre park, and one lonely platform has grown to nearly a dozen permanent stages, including a 23,000-seat amphitheater.

Some of the biggest acts in popular music have played on those stages, for a fraction of the cost to see them elsewhere. Twice, attendance for the festival's 11-day run has topped 1 million people. Even an average year draws more than 800,000 fans.

But Summerfest is more than the sum of its successes. It's the centerpiece of summer in Milwaukee — a place to party, play, shop, eat, drink, dance, people-watch and soak up the sun.

I've been to at least 25 Summerfests, including almost daily visits for the past 18 years as a music writer. Like many native Milwaukeeans, the festival is part of my seasonal mindscape.

Summerfest isn't just a place, it's a state of mind, and it has seeped into and shaped our very identity as a community. For die-hard fans, the first sign of spring in Milwaukee isn't a robin or even the Brewers' Opening Day — it's the first

Dave Tianen has been a music writer for 18 of his 19 years at the Milwaukee Sentinel and the Milwaukee Journal Sentinel.

JOURNAL SENTINEL

MILWAUKEE WORLD FESTIVAL INC

North Gate of Summerfest, date unknown.

JOURNAL SENTINEL

Summerfest concert announcement, usually sometime in March.

Families plan their vacations around the festival. Kids see their first concerts there. Teenagers find their first jobs sweeping the grounds or taking food orders. Friends organize annual reunions around their favorite bands. People meet their future spouses in beer lines or while staking out space on a picnic table.

And surely some old hippies who camped in that muddy field back in 1970 are now taking their grandchildren to frolic on the Summerfest playground.

Think Summerfest, and a kaleidoscope of images springs to mind:

- The Big Bang fireworks echoing beneath the Hoan Bridge on opening night.
- Red, white and blue beach balls bopping around the Marcus Amphitheater at a Jimmy Buffett show.
- Twenty-three thousand people singing along to every song with the BoDeans.
- Middle-age women screaming for Bobby Sherman and Davy Jones.
- Young girls screaming for Chris Brown.
- Fried eggplant strips from the Venice Club.
- Mozzarella marinara sticks from Saz's.
- Bare tummies of every contour.
- Bo Black decked out in Harley gear.

Frank Pachucki danced with his friend, Betty Hornby, both of Milwaukee, in front of the Miller Oasis during a Mt. Olive show on June 25, 1999.

JOURNAL SENTINEL

A fest is **born**

This book is the story of how an abandoned Army missile base became the home of "the world's largest music festival."

Back in 1968, the spot that would become Summerfest was a muddy patch of weeds and concrete, the residence of an obsolete Nike missile base. Aside from the War Memorial Center and the then-Milwaukee Art Center to the north, the surrounding land was bare and undeveloped.

Summerfest took a while to find its identity. In the beginning it was a combination air show, polka fest, car race, film festival and puppet theater scattered among different places all over town.

Its adolescence wasn't without adversity. There was near bankruptcy, a riot, and seven dirty words. At various points through the years the festival had a carnival atmosphere, literally, with freak shows, a midway, a Ferris wheel, fireworks and performing monkeys.

But what has always defined Summerfest is the music.

No other major festival cuts a wider swath through the American songbook. The winds of musical fashion have blown across the grounds: folk, rock, disco, outlaw country, grunge, zydeco, New Age, hip-hop and kiddie pop, to name a few.

Summerfest's stages have been a gathering place for legends. Duke Ellington. Johnny Cash. Bob Hope. Bob Dylan. Van Cliburn. Ella Fitzgerald. Sarah Vaughan. Aretha Franklin, Ray Charles, even a Beatle. The list goes on and on.

Some acts have built good chunks of their careers around Summerfest. Sigmund Snopek III played the festival for 24 years and even wrote a symphony and an opera for it ("Festival World" and "Return of the Spirit," respectively).

According to Summerfest's records, West Coast comedian Will Durst came home for more than 15 summers to play the gig. Waukesha's BoDeans played 18 Summerfests; the Violent Femmes, 13. Jazz trumpeter Maynard Ferguson was a regular at the Miller Oasis (11 years), as was the band Spyro Gyra (14 years). They are featured players in the collected cast of Summerfest.

Parts of the cast have come from the other side of the footlights. Who hasn't seen the graceful couple who waltzed at every stage? Or Peter Rinsky, the retired gentleman who danced with his cane? He was such a familiar sight that festival workers nicknamed him the Stick Man. In 1991, he died at the festival after a long day of dancing.

Even a casual fan can rattle off musical memories:

- Pete Seeger sitting cross-legged, watching on the main stage while Arlo Guthrie sang.
- Tina Turner tearing up the Pabst "oldies" stage in 1983, the year before "Private Dancer" re-ignited her career.
- The amusing culture clash of '60s songbird Lesley Gore and the Indigo Girls at the Big Backyard.
- Fans standing outside the packed Potawatomi Stage straining to hear Lewis Black because they couldn't see him.
- The World Famous Pontani Sisters, in sequined bikinis, dancing with Los Straitjackets.
- Brian Setzer bounding on stage in a leopard-skin suit to "The James Bond Theme."
- Barry's Truckers drinking beer out of a shoe.
- Mayor Henry Maier singing polkas.
- Mayor John Norquist belting out "Blue Suede Shoes."

JOURNAL SENTINEL

A festival-goer admired a model of Milwaukee City Hall made of Legos.

JOURNAL SENTINEL

Cooling off — or is that drinking? — seemed like the right thing to do during one of the three sets Barry's Truckers played at the Pabst Festival Stage in 1984.

Bobby Friss of the Bobby Friss Band came off the stage to perform at the Miller Oasis on July 1, 2000.

A shared legacy

Today, thanks in part to development spurred by Summerfest's success, the lakefront is a thriving recreational destination for Milwaukee and beyond.

The Summerfest grounds, formally known as Maier Festival Park, are surrounded by upscale new neighbors, from the Milwaukee Art Museum's soaring Calatrava addition to the gleaming new Discovery World museum at Pier Wisconsin. There's a new state park to the east on the former "Summerfest island," and the vibrant Historic Third Ward to the west.

Summerfest's influence extends beyond the lakefront. For several years into the late '90s, its companion Winterfest illuminated Cathedral Square and sparked the idea of a downtown ice rink, now in Red Arrow Park.

And we call ourselves the City of Festivals because of the celebrations that sprung up on the Summerfest grounds, from PrideFest in early June to Indian Summer in September. Many of those festivals are now major events in their own right.

But where Summerfest's true legacy lies is in its shared stories.

Do you remember...

• Lining up at midnight to get on a shuttle bus?
• Getting in free with a can of soup?
• Buying a Summerfest sweatshirt to keep warm on a chilly June night?
• Slathering on sunscreen on a blistering July afternoon?
• Seeing Whitney Houston for $12?
• Hearing Bob Dylan and Paul Simon sing "The Wanderer" together?
• Admiring the model of City Hall made of Legos?
• Watching the Truly Remarkable Loon juggle the Machetes of Death?
• Yelling over the roar of dozens of motorcycles revving their engines at closing time?
• Meeting friends under the smiley face balloon?
• Scrambling for free lawn seats at the amphitheater?
• Standing in the rain at the old main stage for the Allman Brothers?
• Sitting on the rocks watching the water ski shows?
• Riding the Sky Glider with the tree tops just below your feet?

Surely there are newcomers and youngsters who will start building their own Summerfest memory book at this year's gig, the 40th staging of the festival.

Some of those experiences will be familiar to all of us, and some of them will be new.

Because Summerfest, like the city it calls home, is a growing, evolving entity — a celebration in motion.

— Dave Tianen

the history

In the beginning, the Smiley Face had a German accent. When it began in 1968, Summerfest was more polka than rock 'n' roll.

I t wasn't centered on the lakefront, and it certainly wasn't expected to become the world's largest music festival. In fact, it wasn't even supposed to be called Summerfest.

The name initially proposed for Summerfest was Juli Spass, a German term meaning "July fun," and early plans for the festival had a definite Germanic cast. Oktoberfest in Munich, Germany, was studied as a possible model for a Milwaukee festival, and it was proposed that one of the planning groups be named for King Gambrinus, the patron saint of brewers. According to legend, Gambrinus once consumed 388 steins of beer at a single setting — a standard rarely threatened by even the heartiest of Summerfest patrons.

The notion of a large Milwaukee festival had been a recurrent idea for much of the city's history. In the summer of 1898, Milwaukee celebrated the 50th anniversary of Wisconsin statehood by hosting a weeklong "Carnival" with sailboat races, parades, band concerts, historical pageants and an illuminated bicycle pageant.

The Civil War battle statuary on Wisconsin Ave. near the public library is a remnant of that event. "Carnival" became an annual event and in 1900 presented Milwaukee with its first parade of horseless carriages. The festival also featured a nighttime parade with 6,000 colored lights. The Milwaukee Sentinel called it "the most beautiful night parade ever planned in America."

"Carnival" was dropped after four years, but in 1933 the idea was revived as the Milwaukee Midsum-

'Think big'

The early powers behind Summerfest in March 1966 (from left): County Executive John Doyne; the festival's first executive director, Willard M. Masterson; festival board president Howard Meister, and Mayor Henry Maier.

Mayor Henry Maier opened Summerfest in 1969 with a song, a toast and some custom apparel.

Gerhard Rudolph led his German band during a noon concert in Carl Zeidler Park at 4th and Michigan streets as part of Summerfest '69. The early years of the festival had a strong Germanic influence.

mer Festival, a lakefront celebration that ran for nine years, until World War II ended it.

The idea of bringing back a summer festival began to circulate in the Milwaukee business community in the late 1950s as a way of drawing tourist dollars to the city. Preliminary plans for an "Augustfest" celebration were made in 1958, but the project fell through when support from local breweries failed to materialize.

The idea was soon revived forcefully with the election of Henry W. Maier as Milwaukee mayor in 1960. The notion of establishing a summer festival was an early initiative of the Maier administration. In 1962, Maier appointed a panel of business and civic leaders to study the feasibility of establishing a

Robert Savage of Chicago spotted balls in the semifinals of the national open lawn bowling tournament held at Lake Park, among the events leading up to the first Summerfest in 1968.

regular summer festival. He encouraged them to "think big."

"I will not be satisfied with anything small scale. I am thinking of an all-out effort, which must not be only a one-shot success but must provide momentum for yearly repeats," he instructed the group.

The mayor proposed a list of suggestions that included concerts by visiting symphony orchestras, an international folk fair, industrial exhibits, a jazz festival, visits by foreign ships, a "little Olympics" and participation by major stars from Hollywood.

He also invoked the city's ethnic heritage: "Milwaukee is unique among American cities in that it still possesses an individual character which most other cities have lost. We have *gemuetlichkeit* — the spirit of good will, which people nationally and internationally associate with us."

Momentum steadily built for the mayor's idea. Gov. Warren Knowles pledged support, calling the proposal good for both the city and the state.

In September 1962, a six-member delegation of business and civic leaders visited Munich, Germany, to gather ideas from that city's Oktoberfest. Upon its return, the group reported Oktoberfest was focused too much on beer for Milwaukee to emulate and recommended a broader cultural focus for a local event. (Summerfest, of course, went on to have breweries sponsor many of its stages).

In April 1964, a mayor's panel submitted a proposal for a 10-day festival that would be coordinated with the Fourth of July Circus Parade, the Milwaukee Art Center art festival and the South Shore Water Frolics.

The group also announced plans to seek sponsorship of a national jazz festival, a national film festival, a national polka festival, a national sculpture show and an international folk fair. Other proposals included powerboat races, dramas to be staged on a showboat on the Milwaukee River, an international flower show, a visiting task force from the U.S. Navy and an international "Ideas Conference" hosting famous intellectuals such as Albert Schweitzer, C.P. Snow and Arnold Toynbee.

The group projected a budget of $300,000 for the event, with the city and the county each contributing $50,000.

As 1965 drew to a close, Willard M. Masterson was hired as the festival's first executive director. Masterson had been administrator of the Wisconsin State Fair since 1951 and was given a starting salary of $22,000 in his new post.

In one of his early statements, Masterson proposed a pageant on the history of Wisconsin, to be staged in County Stadium or Washington Park, with a possible budget as high as $350,000. Masterson was obviously following the mayor's admonition to "think big." Discussing projected attendance for the new festival, he said, "If we don't get a million the first year, we're hardly in business."

A minor bump in the road came in early 1966. The festival had been working under the proposed title Milwaukee World Festival, but in January, the festival board voted to change the name to *Juli Spass* ("July fun"). The group even introduced a new logo with the face of a girl imposed over the sun.

The *Juli Spass* name lasted about two weeks. Irate phone calls poured into radio

Up With People performed at County Stadium three nights during Summerfest '68, including once inside the structure during a storm.

and TV stations and the festival office. Before it even started, the festival had bumped its head on the issue of ethnic diversity. Other nationalities clearly resented giving the new event a Germanic focus.

"Some people who have called have been very hostile," Dorothy Austin, assistant festival director, was quoted as saying. "They've mostly been from the Polish segment of the community."

One caller proposed the title of Fantastic Harlequin Kaleidoscope. Fortunately, at its next meeting the festival board voted for a new name: Summerfest.

Juli Spass Festival

With the name issue resolved, planning and fund-raising continued for the first festival, now slated for July 19 to 28, 1968. More events were announced: an international air show at Mitchell Field, car races at State Fair Park and a national barbershop-quartet singing contest. And in a glimmer of what was to come, a "youth festival" was proposed for the lakefront.

Year one: 1968

The north gate of the Summerfest grounds during the early years.

As you might expect, there were a few more bumps along the way. The late '60s were a time of heightened racial tension in Milwaukee and the nation at large. In 1967, Father James Groppi had begun a series of nightly marches protesting the city's lack of an open-housing ordinance. Violence erupted when Groppi took his marches to the city's south side.

The climate grew more tense when, on the night of July 30, 1967, a riot occurred in Milwaukee's central city. Mayor Maier declared a state of emergency and put the city under a curfew. Rumors circulated that national jazz artists might refuse to come to the city in the wake of the racial tensions.

If it was uneasy, the jazz community wasn't alone. Citing the danger of "civil disturbances," the Army refused permission for the festival to use its 15-acre abandoned lakefront Nike missile site. (Today's grounds include the site of the old missile base.)

In response to the racial tensions spilling over onto festival planning, Maier proposed using Summerfest as an instrument to increase racial understanding. He urged Summerfest to add "a series of events emphasizing the

JOURNAL SENTINEL

A missile stood ready on what would become the permanent Summerfest grounds a few years later.

An aerial view of Summerfest on June 25, 1981.

The TV24 Folk Stage featured Mimi Fariña, James Lee Stanley, Bill Camplin and Corky Siegel in 1980.

Forget rose-colored glasses. This girl was happy to see nothing but the Summerfest Smiley Face logo.

Negro cultural contributions to the nation and this community."

Another disruptive issue arose in February 1968 when director Masterson resigned just five months before the festival was set to launch. Masterson left after announcing he had purchased the Muskego Beach amusement park. Assistant director Austin stepped in as acting director to fill the void.

Eventually it all came off, albeit in a form much different than what we think of Summerfest today.

Summerfest '68 encompassed events in 35 locations. There were puppet shows downtown and a national polka festival in the Auditorium. The Miller 200 stock car race at State Fair Park included a concert starring Rick Nelson, country singer Roy Clark and ventriloquist Jimmy Nelson. The singing group Up With People performed at County Stadium, and a conference on the international status of women was held at Cardinal Stritch University.

There were dramatic readings of Walt Whitman's poetry. Miss USA presided over a "Salute to Milwaukee" dinner at the Pfister Hotel. The Palace Theater hosted an international film festival featuring foreign language films. South African singer Miriam Makeba and band leader Hugh Masekela performed in a "Salute to the African American" at Lincoln and Washington parks. There were nightly fireworks and an air show. The National Ballet of Mexico performed at the Auditorium.

A Youth Fest on the lakefront featured performances by national artists Freddy Cannon, Ronnie Dove and the Robbs, the latter a homegrown band who had gone national

JOURNAL SENTINEL

JOURNAL SENTINEL

Bob Doss of New York tried to attract customers to his game booth at Summerfest on June 27, 1980.

Top: Henry Jordan, then-Summerfest executive director and recently retired Packers defensive lineman, showed some footwork with two folk dancers on what was becoming the Pabst International Festival Stage just weeks before Summerfest '71 opened.

For the 1980 festival, the Pabst stage featured such singers as Sam & Dave, Chubby Checker and ... Mayor Henry Maier (below).

Maier appeared every year at Summerfest to sing, often about the virtures of Milwaukee. He had pushed for a large, recurring festival in the city since the early 1960s.

by landing a spot on Dick Clark's "Where the Action Is" TV show. In a precursor of the popular admission discounts to come, the $1.25 Youth Fest admission was reduced to 50 cents for anyone bringing three 7UP bottle caps.

Youth Fest nearly got blown out over the lake the first day when high winds toppled a tent housing the show. Despite Milwaukee Journal headlines that cried "Screams Pierce Air as Show Tent Falls on Crowd," no one was seriously hurt.

The festival was widely heralded as a success. "Summerfest 68 Receives Bravos, Cries of Encore," read a headline in the Journal. The mayor called the festival a "smashing success" and said he looked forward to an expanded 30-day festival.

Attendance was estimated at more than 1 million, and the event even turned a modest profit of $9,400. There was talk of closing off Wisconsin Ave. and bringing an ocean liner into Milwaukee as a floating hotel during the '69 event.

Always prepared to rise to the occasion musically, Mayor Maier sang for the Washington press corps a new waltz called "The Milwaukee We Know," which he had written to celebrate the city and its festival:

Sweet music falls like a dew,
As fountains spray water at play,
It says, "Dear stranger, to you
We say, have a very good day."
Lights of warmth that are there
Now see the gemuetlichkeit glow
Drifting on musical air
All things in Milwaukee we know.

Rick Nelson sang on the Pabst Festival Stage in 1980.

A clown entertained kids on the Summerfest grounds in 1986.

Chuck Berry — who helped create rock 'n' roll in the 1950s with such seminal classics as "Roll Over Beethoven," "Living In the USA" and "Rock & Roll Music" — performed on the Summerfest main stage on July 23, 1971. Despite a long string of big sellers, Berry would nab his only No. 1 pop chart hit a little more than a year later with "My Ding-A-Ling." He played Summerfest two more times, in 1975 and 1977, also on the main stage.

In many ways, Summerfest '69 was a grander event, with its number of locations nearly doubling to 60.

Bigger in '69

A lmost immediately, the festival got a bonanza of added publicity when Milwaukee police repeatedly arrested a topless maiden performing what was described as a "religious rite" with the Flying Indians of Acapulco.

The vice squad obviously had untapped a hidden reservoir of spiritual curiosity in the community. Soon the Flying Indians were drawing crowds estimated at more than 20,000. Eventually, spirituality triumphed when a court order blocked the police from making further arrests.

Bigger names were booked for the festival. Bob Hope played two shows at County Stadium. B.B. King, Wilson Pickett and the Staple Singers played the Arena.

But cold, wet weather plagued the festival for much of its run from July 18 to 27. The festival's final day was completely washed out, with the events canceled due to inclement weather. Summerfest '69 closed its books $164,000 in debt. Clearly, the very survival of the festival was at stake.

A committee of local business members led by Pfister Hotel President Ben Marcus was formed to save Summerfest. The immediate crisis was resolved when John Kelly, owner and president of Midland National Bank, offered the festival an unsecured loan of $175,000. Eventually pledges from sponsors and area businesses brought in $280,000 to help buoy the struggling celebration.

And in a move of lasting significance, the festival also transferred its offices to buildings on the former Army Nike base on the lakefront and worked out a deal to lease the property from the Harbor Commission for $1 a year.

Summerfest 1970 was clearly going to be a pivotal year. For the first time, events would

JOURNAL SENTINEL

Ten acres of parking lots near the main stage were landscaped in 1981 to hold a concession stand and fountain as part of the Summerfest grounds.

JOURNAL SENTINEL

The main stage area at the north end of the grounds was crowded with festivalgoers wanting to hear the Charlie Daniels Band and Dickey Betts on July 1, 1982.

Will Durst got laughs at the Comedy Cabaret on July 4, 1990.

The venerable Pete Seeger (left) and Arlo Guthrie sang folk songs on the main stage on July 2, 1980.

be concentrated on the site of the present grounds rather than spread around the city. Work had begun to transform the former lakefront Nike base, with its concrete missile emplacements, into a more festive environment.

The festival also had a new executive director. In March, recently retired Green Bay Packer tackle Henry Jordan, 35, was named the acting director. That year the festival also adopted the familiar smiley face logo that has been its symbol ever since.

Although its lakefront stage was still a temporary structure built on concrete blocks, Summerfest 1970 was a stunning comeback.

It was also taking on the character of the big, diverse musical festival we know today. According to police estimates, a July 26 performance by Sly & the Family Stone drew a massive crowd of between 100,000 and 125,000 — a wildly improbable number given the space involved, festival officials later said. Crowd size not withstanding, the Sly & the Family Stone show entered Summerfest folklore as a kind of Brew City Woodstock.

Other A-list names to play the festival that year included James Brown, Sarah Vaughan, Chicago, Jose Feliciano, Bobby Sherman and Pat Paulsen. When it was done, attendance at the 10-day event was again estimated at more than 1 million. The Milwaukee Sentinel wrote: "Although the death rattle was sounded after last year's festival, this year Summerfest '70 sprang back with surprising vitality."

The grounds were still largely undeveloped. As then-alderman and later Summerfest board member Bill Drew recalls, fest-goers were up to their ankles in mud when it rained and up to their ankles in dust when it didn't.

Bob Milkovich, who ran the Pabst stage for many years, recalls a wet and smelly locale in those early days.

"I remember I did the Miss Milwaukee Summerfest Pageant," he says. "It was right after the Schlitz Parade. You've got the elephant smell. You've got the horse smell. They had the pageant in a tent. We literally had to spray the tent with disinfectant so that elephant smell would go away."

And that was in good weather. When it rained, he says, "in front of the stage was the Milkovich Lake. It was about 25 square feet, with six inches of water. It smelled like hell."

JOURNAL SENTINEL

The overhead Sky Glider — shown on June 29, 1997 — has provided an easy way to traverse the Summerfest grounds without getting caught in the crowds.

The Miller Jazz Oasis featured Roy Buchanan, Buddy Rich, Sonny Rollins and Chick Corea in 1978. Note the tableclothes.

Milwaukee native Al Jarreau sang on the main stage on June 30, 1984.

Coming off a 1970 profit of $167,000, Summerfest '71 expanded its entertainment lineup.

The main stage's roster included the Jackson 5, Blood, Sweat & Tears, B.B. King with Muddy Waters and Paul Butterfield, a country package featuring Roy Clark and Ray Price, and a rock 'n' roll revival anchored by Little Richard and Chuck Berry.

The Miller High Life Jazz Oasis made its bow with shows by Buddy Montgomery and Milwaukee jazz guitarist George Pritchett, among others. Attendance was projected at 40% over the previous year's turnout.

In truth, early Summerfest attendance estimates probably should be taken with a grain of skepticism. Nobody really knew how big the crowds were; the festival didn't introduce turnstiles until 1983. Summerfest initially relied on police crowd estimates and later turned to weighing admission tickets.

Police crowd estimates sometimes exceeded the physical capacity of the site by seven or eight times. Regardless of the actual numbers, after just four years of operation, Summerfest was able to claim a ranking among the five biggest festivals in the country.

Summerfest '72 will always be remembered as the year the Summerfest smile got its mouth washed out with soap. On July 21, comedian George Carlin opened on the main stage for folkie Arlo Guthrie and repeated his bit on the "Seven Words You Can't Say on Television." Carlin had already done the Seven Words on a comedy album and performed them without incident at the John F. Kennedy Center for the Performing Arts in Washington, D.C., but the same police department that had protected Milwaukee from the topless woman in the Flying Indians of Acapulco had not relaxed its vigilance. Milwaukee police arrested Carlin and charged him with disorderly conduct after he left the stage.

No fool, Carlin recognized a valuable publicity opportunity when he was given one. He promptly branded the offending words the Milwaukee Seven and repeated the story

The 'Seven Words'

JOURNAL SENTINEL

Saturday, July 22, 1972, edition

JOURNAL SENTINEL ARCHIVES

Comedian George Carlin made headlines (and police mug shots) for his Summerfest '72 performance by saying seven naughty words.

An anxious opening day crowd expecting a storm waited for the Allman Brothers Band to take the main stage on the first night of the 1979 festival. It began to rain a short time later. It was the first show at the "new" old main stage with the large curved roof.

on "The Dick Cavett Show." Eventually, a Milwaukee judge dismissed the charges, and Carlin even repeated the entire bit with three new words at the Riverside Theater the next year without managing to get arrested.

At the time, though, Summerfest Executive Director Jordan was profusely apologetic.

"I had no idea he was like that," Jordan was quoted as saying in the Milwaukee Sentinel. "I have seen him many times on the Johnny Carson show, and I had no idea he would use that kind of vulgarity. Summerfest is supposed to be a family show."

Despite a violent storm that forced evacuation of the grounds on opening day, Summerfest '72 still drew more than 500,000 people and was able to make a small profit. That year also saw the beginning of the Summerfest marketplace, which had grown from a mere flea market with a rock stage. Another major brewery sponsor also joined the party with the Tent Theater supported by the Jos. Schlitz Brewing Co. The tent featured performances by the Milwaukee Repertory Theater.

A storm moved through the Summerfest grounds on July 2, 1978, forcing the cancellation of several acts, including a main stage concert by the Grateful Dead.

Although its fiscal problems had apparently been resolved, the festival would soon face a crisis of a different kind.

'Stay away from rock groups'

Summerfest had moved far away from Mayor Maier's vision of a family-friendly polka party, and in 1973 the hard-rocking bash got out of hand.

The newspaper headlines told the story:

"Police Battle Crowds at Summerfest"

"Pandemonium Erupts at Summerfest"

"Wave of Arrests Inundates Jail"

"Officials Undaunted by Festival Melee"

On the next-to-last night of the festival, a main stage performance by the rock band Humble Pie turned ugly when fans stormed a beer tent, smashed beer barrels, pried open locked refrigerators, tore down beer stands and tossed folding chairs into a half-dozen bonfires. Police in riot gear waded into the unruly crowd, and in the resulting brawl approximately 300 fans were arrested. So many people were taken into custody that city jails were swamped by the deluge.

A story in the Milwaukee Journal described the aftermath: "In the north end of the grounds nothing remained but beer cans, broken glass and the remains of destroyed refreshment stands. Debris was about six inches deep. A large part of the main stage was torn off and fed to the bonfires."

Musician Sigmund Snopek III was there that day and remembers that it wasn't safe even backstage.

"I saw a brick hit (entertainment director) Shila Boyd. A brick came over the wall and hit her right in the side of the head. It was pretty intense," recalls Snopek, who was backstage because the festival had rented his Marshall amps. "They wanted to get free beer. That was the climate of the day... . It was just a violent night."

"They broke into a beer truck," Milkovich recalls. "It started from the north end... . It was very scary, very scary. If somebody said, 'How did it start?' I'd have no idea."

The Humble Pie riot forced Summerfest management to reassess what the festival was and who it was meant to serve.

JOURNAL SENTINEL

Jeff Reiter danced with his wife, Amy, to the music of the R&B Cadets on July 1, 2003.

Monday, July 23, 1973, edition

Helen Reddy sang at the main stage on the north end of the grounds on July 4, 1978. The "banana" or "Dolly Parton" roof was replaced the following year by an arched roof (see page 28).

MILWAUKEE WORLD FESTIVAL INC

In the immediate aftermath, Jordan said, "If I'm going to have anything to do with it, we definitely will stay away from rock groups."

Mayor Maier urged a return to the ethnic, family-style celebration he had originally envisioned.

"When we allowed it to get the atmosphere it did in the past we made a very big mistake," he said. "We are the ethnic capital of North America. I hope we can place greater emphasis on the festival as the hub of America."

Although the festival never returned to Maier's polka-fest vision, there was a definite shift toward less volatile pop, folk and country acts. The headliners in 1974 included Doc Severinsen, Peter Nero and the Milwaukee Symphony, Helen Reddy, the O'Jays, Mela-

nie with Harry Chapin, Charley Pride and nostalgic rock act Sha Na Na.

The Humble Pie riot, however, masked the genuine progress that Summerfest was continuing to make. A new 10-year lease, with the festival continuing to pay $1 a year for rent, was negotiated with the Harbor Commission, allowing the festival to begin construction of more permanent facilities on the grounds. Besides the shift in musical direction, Summerfest '74 introduced two new stages to go with the Miller Jazz Oasis and the rock stage: the Schlitz Country stage, which hosted Earl Scruggs and Tanya Tucker, and the Pabst International Folk Festival.

Another important step in the evolution of the modern festival took place in 1975 when

Summerfest opened up its food vending operations to area restaurants. The change greatly diversified the food at the festival and created a revenue stream that eventually became Summerfest's leading source of income.

Although Summerfest never became the ethnic-focused event Maier seemed to prefer, the mayor's vision was realized with the rise of the weekend ethnic festivals on the Summerfest grounds, which gave Milwaukee legitimate claim to the name "City of Festivals." Festa Italiana and Mexican Fiesta debuted in 1978, followed by German Fest and Irish Fest three years later and Polish Fest in 1982.

Summerfest suffered an unexpected blow on Feb. 21, 1977, when executive director Henry Jordan died of a heart attack after jogging at the Milwaukee Athletic Club. He was only 42 and had headed the festival since 1970. As a perennial all-pro and a member of the Super Bowl-winning Packer teams of the '60s, Jordan had given Summerfest a touch of celebrity sports glamour. But he was also a dedicated manager who slept on the grounds during the festival run and helped

The Summerfest grounds as seen from the Marcus Amphitheater.

Identical twins, Jenna (left) and Julie Tellefsen, then 16, enjoyed wearing matching Summerfest sweatshirts and shopping for hair extensions at the festival in 2005.

A city of festivals

Debuts of annual lakefront festivals on the Summerfest grounds:

1978: Festa Italiana and Mexican Fiesta

1981: German Fest and Irish Fest

1982: Polish Fest

1983: African World Festival (started as AfroFest)

1987: Indian Summer

1996: PrideFest *

1994-2005: Asian Moon

1998: Arab World Festival (started as Arabian Fest)

* Pride Celebration debuted in 1988, moved to East Town in 1989, was re-named PrideFest in 1991 and moved to the Summerfest grounds in 1996.

The 5th Dimension sang at Summerfest in the early '80s.

Then-Summerfest director Rod Lanser held a monkey that appeared at the festival in 1980.

guide Summerfest to steady profitability after a rocky beginning.

Snopek has fond memories of Jordan.

"Henry Jordan was a dynamic man to work for," he says. "I remember I wanted to get a new truck, and I needed to ask him for a $500 advance. I had never asked for an advance before in my life. . . .

"I was really nervous. This was Henry Jordan, the guy who played for the Packers, a legend. He was a lot of fun. He said, 'Sure, Sig. I'll have 'em write you a check right now.' That's when I realized you could get advances.

"He was dynamic and fun, and the people who worked for him just loved him."

After a national search for a new executive director, the festival board settled on former WISN-TV general manager James T. Butler.

Butler had served on the Summerfest executive committee for seven years, had close ties with Mayor Maier and was familiar with the festival and the community. On the other hand, he was widely regarded as a hard-line, even abrasive, executive and had been fired by WISN.

Butler's tenure was short. He resigned in October 1979 after months of speculation that his combative style had alienated the Summerfest executive board.

"There are two things I remember about Jim," recalls Tracy Spoerl, the festival's director of concessions. "He was a very stern taskmaster. He watched the bottom line, and he was excellent at that. You didn't order a roll of toilet paper without his approving it … but I think that really helped us. In the early years when Summerfest struggled financially it was important to have somebody at the helm who was sensitive to the spending.

"After 5 o'clock he was a delightful man. You never heard the same joke twice. He was a great storyteller."

One important addition during Butler's tenure was the hiring of Bob Babisch. A former booking agent with the local Edgewood Talent Agency, Sheboygan native Babisch joined the staff in 1977 as a stage manager and rose to entertainment director the next year. He's been there ever since, and as the man responsible for booking the festival's entertainment, he has been the leading force in shaping Summerfest as a major music event.

For Butler's replacement, Summerfest turned to a familiar and popular figure in Milwaukee politics: Ald. Rod Lanser. A former salesman, the silver-haired Lanser was considered a strong booster of the Milwaukee community and was closely allied with Mayor Maier.

The issues facing Summerfest in the late '70s and early '80s were largely the complica-

Jamila Warner, 8, of Milwaukee, enjoyed the Summerfest merry-go-round on June 30, 1993.

Amanda Gilbert and Steven Krause, both of Milwaukee and then 17, relaxed during Summerfest 2001.

A common sight at Summerfest is table dancing. Doris Kallow watched three dancers enjoy music at the Miller Oasis on June 28, 2001.

tions of success: finding parking, upgrading the grounds, building attendance and finding the right balance of family and contemporary entertainment.

In 1975, a comedy stage joined the roster, featuring the likes of David Brenner and John Byner; the next year an emerging comic named Billy Crystal made his Summerfest debut. The established stages continued to evolve as well, with the Pabst International Festival stage moving from a world music focus to an oldies-rock format in 1978. With the festival on solid financial footing in 1977, the City of Milwaukee suspended its cash contributions.

Summerfest in the late '70s and early '80s was clearly intent on preserving its family image, even if it meant avoiding high-drawing but potentially troublesome rock acts. The main stage bookings in that era veered heavily toward country, pop and adult R&B. The lineup for 1978, for example, was Boz Scaggs, the Bar-Kays, Dolly Parton, Bobby Vinton, the Marshall Tucker Band, Helen Reddy, Journey, Waylon Jennings, the O'Jays, Willie Nelson with Emmylou Harris, and Mac Davis. A scheduled date with the Grateful Dead was washed out by a storm.

"We're no longer a rock festival," Lanser said in 1981. "I think we could have capacity crowds on the main stage every night if we wanted to. Just book rock bands. But we don't want to. We're more concerned about image."

Britney Spears:
Marcus Amphitheater
July 8, 2000

Beer drinkers lined up at the Leinenkugel tent in 2001.

A vivid rainbow encompassed the festival grounds as the crowd waited out a short rain in 2003.

Leann Hoople (left) and Rachel Nelson told their friends about the shows they had been seeing at the U.S. Cellular stage during the 2005 festival.

Bo Black oversaw Summerfest as its director for nearly 20 years, turning a regional event into "the world's largest music festival."

Summerfest entered a new era in 1983 when Lanser unexpectedly resigned, citing job stress and health concerns. His replacement was a former (clothed) Playboy cover girl, NFL cheerleader, mayoral aide and professional fund-raiser named Elizabeth "Bo" Black.

Black, 37, knew how to shake the money tree. Working on behalf of Maier, she had assembled the largest pre-election war chest in Milwaukee political history, even though the mayor was unopposed. Black's relative youth and good looks may have been deceiving. Contemporary press accounts quoted unnamed insiders as predicting Black "wouldn't dominate the festival as Lanser had."

So much for insider insight.

Black's first Summerfest as executive director was in 1984, and she went on to oversee Summerfest for nearly 20 years, building it from a firmly established regional event into "the world's largest music festival." Her talent as a fund-raiser drew sponsor support that allowed the festival to grow while still remaining readily affordable for families.

In 1984 Summerfest was bringing in $542,000 in sponsorship money. By 1996 that figure had risen to $4 million. The many grounds improvements and the modest admission prices at Summerfest would not have been possible without Black's fund-raising efforts.

"She could raise money where nobody else could," recalls Bill Drew, who was on the Summerfest board from 1974 to 1988. "A very prominent businessman told me one time that he deals with fund-raisers all the time, but the one that he really hates to see coming is Bo because she always gets what she wants."

Black took particular pride in the many promotions that allowed patrons to enter Summerfest at little or no cost. She also took seriously the mission to provide employment

The Bo Black era

Huey Lewis and Bo Black

The Summerfest Mid-gate, circa 1990.

MILWAUKEE WORLD FESTIVAL INC

The Beach Boys — including Brian Wilson and Mike Love (second and third, from left) — were the first act to perform on the Marcus Amphitheater stage, on June 25, 1987.

Crowds poured into the Marcus Amphitheater during Summerfest '89.

for minority children through her Operation Summer Chance program.

Perhaps most important, Black was a vivid personality and glamorous presence who gave the festival a readily identifiable public face. In an era when female chief executives were still rare, she was the most visible CEO in town. She was arguably Milwaukee's most popular celebrity, and to much of the public, she was Summerfest. She was also a colorful and sometimes eccentric boss. If there was something on her mind, her staff might get calls in the middle of the night.

Vic Thomas, Summerfest's assistant entertainment director, recalls a determined and hard-driving executive: "She was somebody who when something was on her mind, it was on her mind. I guess that's a real attribute for somebody that's a fund-raiser.... She was tenacious. If she wanted something, it became a company priority."

Black's early tenure was not exactly headache-free. Actually, there were some tummy aches, too. In 1985, the city Health Department ordered the water supply at the festival shut off twice for a span of several days because of possible bacterial contamination. Approximately 90 people reported stomach upsets after visiting the festival. With the water fountains shut off, Summerfest substituted about 4,000 gallons of bottled water for patrons to drink. Although the problem cleared up, the source of the contamination was never found.

The '80s were a time of dramatic site development at Summerfest. Paved walkways replaced what had been gravel paths. Food vendors were given new permanent structures. Bathroom facilities were expanded. In 1983, turnstiles were introduced, giving

Summerfest much more reliable attendance data. There were new stages such as Leinie's Lodge and a new comedy pavilion on the south end of the grounds. And the biggest change of all was the opening of the $12 million, 23,000-seat Marcus Amphitheater in 1987.

The new amphitheater was built on filled land on the south end of the grounds and funded through the sale of bonds plus a $1 million gift from the Marcus family and a $2 million donation from the G. Heileman Brewing Co. Seating in the new venue was a combination of 9,000 reserved seats and 14,000 bench and lawn seats.

Despite a threatened lawsuit and a strike by construction workers, the new facility opened to rave reviews. The Milwaukee Journal said, "The amphitheater ... turned out to be everything Summerfest officials hoped it would." The Milwaukee Sentinel praised the amphitheater's "superb acoustics."

The addition of reserved seats provided a new revenue stream — many seats were from $5 to $10 — and gave Summerfest the heft to bring in truly A-list talent. The first-year line-up in the new amphitheater was one of the most glittering in festival history, including Paul Simon on his "Graceland" tour, new R&B singing sensation Whitney Houston, rap pioneers Run-DMC, plus Duran Duran, Jimmy Buffett, Chicago, the Beach Boys, Dolly Parton, the Bangles, Bruce Hornsby and John Denver.

And the amphitheater allowed Summerfest to continue drawing top-flight attractions. Many of the most glittering names of the '90s and '00s would eventually play there, including Pearl Jam, Shania Twain, Britney Spears,

The Marcus Amphitheater offered the fest's first reserved seats. Before then, all shows, even the main stage, were included in the price of admission to the grounds.

A midway with rides and carnival booths was a staple at Summerfest for many years. The midway was discontinued after 2002.

Gwen Stefani (with No Doubt), Dave Matthews, Metallica, Christina Aguilera, Kenny Chesney and Mary J. Blige.

The 1987 celebration also marked the final bow of the man acknowledged as the Father of Summerfest, Mayor Henry Maier. The retiring mayor visited the grounds and led a sing-along that included two songs of his own composition, "The Milwaukee Summerfest Polka" and "Mayor Maier's Farewell," written specifically for the occasion. At the end of 1986 the Summerfest board had voted unanimously to rename the festival grounds Henry W. Maier Festival Park.

For his farewell visit, the mayor repeated his often-stated view of the Summerfest mission: "The ordinary guy in Milwaukee and outside of Milwaukee, who did not have a membership in a country club or didn't have a country home on a lake, needed a place to go and things to do in the summertime."

Keeping Summerfest accessible for Maier's "ordinary guy" was a major priority of the Bo Black regime. In 1990, the festival reinstituted its original 1970 Summerfest Pin promotion, which allowed buyers to get into the festival free during weekday afternoons. Since the pins were sold in the weeks before the festival opened, they also provided Summerfest with a revenue buffer against the potential of lower attendance because of bad weather. A survey in 1997 found that 21% of Summerfest attendees used some kind of discount to purchase their admission. For instance, festival promotions for 1995 included Rayovac Day, Alka Mints Day, Big T Day and M&M/Mars Day.

The 1980s and '90s were years of steady attendance growth for the festival. In 1983, using its new turnstiles, Summerfest counted its attendance at 657,429. In 2001, after years of growth, attendance at Summerfest officially passed the million mark for the first time. Helping fuel the growth was a sellout of the entire 120,000 run of Summerfest pins.

The '90s also witnessed continued modernization and development of the grounds. In 1994 the North Gate was redesigned, the Leinie Lodge got a new, permanent stage at the Koss Pavilion, and the Potawatomi Bingo Casino/V100 Soul Stage made its debut.

A major hurdle in the continued growth of Summerfest was passed with the negotiation of a new lease in 2001 that secured the festival's position on the lakefront for 20 years while dramatically increasing its annual rent payments.

Under a 1985 agreement, Summerfest had been paying $1 year in rent plus 2% of its net income, approximately $30,000 a year. The 2001 deal raised the rent to roughly $1 million a year. But even with the new rent scale in place, Summerfest 2001 still managed a healthy $2.3 million profit.

However, the lease agreement revealed tensions within the Summerfest family that undermined Bo Black's once unassailable position as executive director. After the city and Summerfest board reached agreement on the new lease, Black publicly criticized the deal in a radio interview, saying it would deplete the festival's reserves and leave it vulnerable to a run of bad weather. Adding to the tension, Black had publicly feuded with Mayor John Norquist for years.

Signs that Black's position had dramatically eroded were evident when the board declined to take up the matter of her contract extension at its December 2002 meeting. In September 2003, the Summerfest board voted to dismiss Black, bringing an end to her 19-year tenure as the public face of Summerfest.

Summerfest annexes winter

In the 1990s, Summerfest expanded its seasonal reach by taking over Winterfest. The Summerfest staff ran the downtown festival from 1991 through 1997-'98. Although centered at Cathedral Square, the festival was a throwback to the earliest days of Summerfest, with events scattered around downtown. At its peak Winterfest included a comedy festival that included such names as Chris Rock, Judy Tenuta and Rich Hall, concerts by acts like Buckwheat Zydeco and Duran Duran, ice sculpting contests and an ice rink in Cathedral Square.

The comedy festival was housed in the cafeteria of the former St. John's Cathedral School, an arrangement that became awkward when the frisky adult content of Tenuta's comedy offended the sensibilities of the parish priest. In an effort to smooth things over, Summerfest posted signs in the dressing room warning the comedians not to use X-rated language — a warning that Chris Rock effectively demolished in the first 30 seconds of his act.

Although Winterfest escaped eviction, it never became a profitable enterprise. Milwaukee World Festival Inc., the non-profit corporation that runs Summerfest, ceased operating Winterfest after 1997-'98, although the festival did spark enthusiasm for a downtown ice rink, now at Red Arrow Park.

As a replacement, the board turned to veteran baseball executive Don Smiley, named president and CEO of Milwaukee World Festival Inc., the non-profit corporation that runs Summerfest, in April 2004. A native of Racine, Smiley had been president of the Florida Marlins baseball team and an executive with Blockbuster Entertainment. With dramatically increased rent, an aging patron base, escalating entertainment costs and a $50 million capital improvement plan, Smiley said his priority would be finding ways to increase Summerfest revenue.

After topping a million in attendance two years in a row, in 2001 and 2002, Summerfest experienced several consecutive years of declining attendance. The slump was reversed in 2005 when attendance rebounded to 901,841, up 4%. The festival also saw a 12% increase in revenue.

The 2006 festival saw the festival take on a major project: the replacement of Summerfest's oldest stage, the Miller Lite Oasis. At a cost of $2.5 million, Miller Brewing Co. rebuilt the stage facing east, nearly doubling the capacity of the viewing area from 6,000 to 11,000 and creating the first Summerfest grounds stage to feature projection TV screens. Another addition in 2006 was a partnership with African World Festival that created a gospel music contest among area church choirs; the festival has periodically been criticized for not having enough entertainment that appeals to African-Americans.

While it has grown dramatically from the lawn bowling, puppet show, car race, polka fest of its beginnings, Summerfest continues to honor Mayor Maier's original vision of a celebration accessible to all of Milwaukee's citizens. General admission, which includes access to everything except most amphitheater shows, was $15 in 2006.

"In the big picture, we have the best music festival out there," Smiley says. "It really does offer something for everyone. . . . When you go around the country and look at what tickets cost, Summerfest has remained very affordable. We intend to keep it that way."

Donald A. Smiley, president and chief executive officer of Milwaukee World Festival Inc.

JOURNAL SENTINEL

the music

Maynard Ferguson played to a full house for two nights at the Miller Jazz Oasis to kick off Summerfest in 1988.

Summerfest is all things to all ears — or at least, it tries to be.
Of the major American music festivals, none paints with as broad a brush.

The New Orleans Jazz & Heritage Festival celebrates the sound of the Crescent City. Bonnaroo is heavy on jam bands and roots music. Coachella is a rock festival. Fan Fair is a country music meet-and-greet on a grand scale. There's a Newport festival for jazz, and one for folk.

But with nearly a dozen stages and an 11-day run, Summerfest is bigger, longer and more musically diverse.

Consider the lineup for just one year: 1991. Playing the Marcus Amphitheater during the festival's 11 days were the hair metal band Warrant, Spanish crooner Julio Iglesias, rowdy country rocker Hank Williams Jr., Jimmy Buffett and his parrotheads, urban music stylists Bell Biv DeVoe, mom-and-daughter country harmony act the Judds, rock group Tesla, bar-band-gone-platinum Huey Lewis & the News, blue-eyed soul man Mi-

Previous page: A leaping Eddie Vedder and Pearl Jam open the Marcus Amphitheater for Tom Petty & the Heartbreakers on the first day of Summerfest 2006.

Carlos Santana (left) leads Santana at the Marcus on July 3, 2005.

SUMMERFEST

47

MILWAUKEE WORLD FESTIVAL INC.

Dolly Parton brought country pop to the Marcus Amphitheater on June 28, 1987. She first performed at Summerfest in 1969 when festival events were being held all over the city and she was still part of Porter Wagoner's show, which played the Arena with Tex Ritter opening.

Glen Campbell sang on the main stage on July 14, 1972.

MILWAUKEE WORLD FESTIVAL INC.

chael Bolton, acoustic punksters the Violent Femmes and R&B diva Whitney Houston.

And that was just the main stage. The grounds stages that year included Michael McDonald, Spyro Gyra, The Band, the Fabulous Thunderbirds, Albert King, Davy Jones, Eddie Money, the Replacements, the Four Seasons, Buckwheat Zydeco, Dr. John, Koko Taylor, Marshall Tucker, the Commodores, the Rippingtons, the Temptations, the DiVinyls, Kansas, Blue Oyster Cult, Leon Russell, the Dirty Dozen Brass Band, Elvin Bishop, Paula Poundstone, Emo Philips, Otis Rush, Richard Elliot and Junior Wells.

Because Summerfest has been a centerpiece of the local culture for so long, it's easy to forget what a truly remarkable variety of music and entertainment it brings to Milwaukee each year.

It wasn't always that way.

Although diverse, the first Summerfest

wasn't focused on bringing big-name entertainment to Milwaukee. The largest share of pre-festival publicity went to a polka festival held at the Arena.

The biggest concert of Summerfest '68 was an appearance by the troupe Up With People at County Stadium. Rock and Roll Hall of Famer Rick Nelson played the fairgrounds, but that show was mainly just an add-on to the Miller 200 car race. In 1968, Nelson was well past his teen idol days of the '50s and before his "Garden Party" comeback in 1972.

But by Summerfest '69, there was already a slight shift toward the kind of national entertainment that the festival would soon feature. The Bob Seger System, the Box Tops, Brooklyn Bridge and the 1910 Fruitgum Company all played the lakefront. There was a country show at the Arena with a young Dolly Parton when she was still partnered with Porter Wagoner. The pop piano duo of Ferrante & Teicher played Washington Park. There was also what must have been a splashy soul and blues show at the Arena with B.B. King, Wilson Pickett and the Staple Singers.

The performance that got the most attention, however,

JOURNAL SENTINEL

Aretha Franklin on the main stage June 30, 1981, after the Four Tops opened.

JOURNAL SENTINEL

was easily a pair of shows at County Stadium by comedy icon Bob Hope. Even Hope's arrival at Mitchell Field got major feature treatment in both Milwaukee newspapers.

The Sentinel headlined: "Bob Hope Electrifies Audience." Not surprisingly, Hope offered his take on the recent Apollo moon landing. "This is one of our most successful government projects — we spent $24 billion and got 80 pounds of rocks." There was also some evidence of the "generation gap" in Hope's jokes poking fun at hippies. "I saw a kid with hair so long he had to cut arm holes in it," he said.

Sly and the 'Seven Words'

The early years of Summerfest produced two of its defining moments — shows that people still talk about to this day, even if they only know about them through word of mouth.

Although it only featured one stage, Summerfest '70 was notable as the first year the festival was held on the lakefront site that became its permanent home. It also marked the shift to a big-name menu of national music acts with a lineup that included James Brown, Sarah Vaughan, Chicago, Pat Paulsen with Jose Feliciano, Doc Severinsen, and teen idols Bobby Sherman and Andy Kim.

The show that went down in Summerfest folklore, however, was an overflow crowd for

Sly & the Family Stone.

Much of the news coverage focused on the sheer size of the event. Police crowd estimates ran from 100,000 to 125,000. The Milwaukee Journal wrote that "if they had all stood up, held hands and formed a circle, they could have surrounded Milwaukee." The Milwaukee Sentinel reported that the "marijuana smoke was so thick in the area that if there had been a shift in the wind, a good share of the community of Grand Rapids, Michigan, might have gotten stoned."

According to the Sentinel, even Sly was scared by the crowd size and only consented to leave the Pfister Hotel when Summerfest provided three limos. As it was, Sly went on at least an hour late, and local deejays Bob Reitman and O.C. White spent much of the night trying to keep the crowd calm.

Sporadic fights and mere crowd pressure in the muddy field gave the night a definite edge.

"O.C. White was backstage," Reitman recalls. "He was basically emcee-ing the show. I was sort of there as. . . the token hippie.

"The stage was only a couple feet off the ground, and the only protection between the crowd and the stage was a snow fence, to the best of my memory. They were jammed in, and there were a lot of people there. . . . It was a huge crowd. . . . As time went along, they got more and more restless. . . .

"At a certain point O.C. took me by the arm and said, 'We're going to go out there. . .' O.C. started to tell the crowd to relax and calm down, and things like that. The vivid memory I have is that eventually everybody sat down except for one woman. . . She was standing there screaming at O.C. It was a showdown between the two of them, and O.C. prevailed. She finally sat down.

JOURNAL SENTINEL

He was never elected president, but comedian Pat Paulsen campaigned for laughs at the Lakefront Stage on July 17, 1970.

JOURNAL SENTINEL

Andy Kim sang at Summerfest's Lakefront Stage on July 22, 1970, opening for another pop heartthrob, Bobby Sherman.

Little Richard belted out songs from atop a grand piano as he electrified the main stage audience on July 23, 1971.

"It was scary, and it was really annoying at the time. You had a huge crowd like that, that was really upset. O.C. did a great job of talking that crowd down. On the other hand, it was: Where the hell is this guy (Sly)? What's he doing? Once he showed up, people calmed down."

While acknowledging that most fans were well-behaved, the Journal wrote: "There were enough troublemakers, reckless types and just plain dumbheads to dim the luster of the attendance figure and turn Summerfest's last night into a cultural and behavioral letdown." The writers for both papers treated the show itself almost as an after-thought.

As it turned out, things could have been much worse. Not long after Summerfest, Sly also played the same delaying game for a free concert in Chicago's Grant Park. According to Time magazine, in the resulting three-hour melee police fired their weapons, 160 people were arrested and more than 150 people, including 91 officers, were injured.

JOURNAL SENTINEL ARCHIVE

George Carlin

Another Summerfest legend was created in 1972. The festival found itself in the national limelight when comedian George Carlin was arrested for disorderly conduct after performing his "Seven Words You Can't Say on Television" on the main stage.

The comic's set was a little rocky even before the arrest. After coming out, Carlin, who was opening for Arlo Guthrie, told the audience that the crowd might be too big for him to establish a rapport. His microphone went dead after the Seven Words bit, and twice a woman climbed on stage and began yelling at him to get off.

Later, Carlin told a Milwaukee Journal reporter that he thought the crowd would be made up of strictly younger people. Apparently his anti-Vietnam War material and attacks on the hypocrisy of American drug laws went over well enough with most of the crowd. The officer in charge of the Summerfest police detail was reported to have said that he decided to arrest the comedian after getting angry complaints from several parents who attended the show with their children.

Bo Diddley played the main stage as part of a six-act rock 'n' roll show on July 23, 1971.

Luther Allison opened for B.B. King, Muddy Waters and the Paul Butterfield Blues Band for a main stage "blues night" on July 20, 1971.

Oh, those **Summerfest nights**

Although Summerfest offers acts for people of all ages, the promise of live music and hours of hanging out have always made the festival a magnet for young people. But just getting to the isolated, underdeveloped site was something of a quest in the early days.

Vic Thomas, Summerfest's current assistant entertainment director, remembers trudging to the lakefront on foot as a teenager before the buses came close — anything to get down to the grounds.

"I remember the first time I came to Summerfest. It would have been 1972," he says. "I remember I was hav-

James Pankow of the rock group Chicago wailed away on the Marcus Amphitheater stage on July 3, 1987.

ing such a good time, and the buses had stopped running when it ended. I got in so much trouble with my folks. I had to walk from here to my house, which was on 19th and Hadley. At the time I was 14, maybe 15 years old.

"I had my first date down here, which I will always remember. . . . The girl drove; I didn't know how to drive. . . She had this beautiful pants suit on, and that was a time when it was muddy, with all the wood chips. She was a mess, but it was one of those memories."

The sheer size of Summerfest accommodates all manner of attack plans. Some fans just turn out for the big-ticket event in the amphitheater. Many others pledge allegiance to a particular grounds stage and camp there for the duration. They might annex the same picnic table year after year.

Still others bounce around the grounds, playing musical pinball, catching an elder blues statesman at one stage, a local cover outfit at another and a slice of African pop at yet another. And still others find their kicks reuniting with a favorite act that returns

Waylon Jennings (left) performed on the main stage on July 10, 1976. Summerfest definitely liked him as a main stage act: He was booked to play there in '78, '79 and '80 but canceled the last two times.

year after year. Those are the people who look forward each summer to bonding with Sigmund Snopek over a chorus of "Thank God This Isn't Cleveland" or watching to see if trumpeter Maynard Ferguson finally blows a hole in the roof of the Miller Oasis with one of his signature high notes.

Veteran Milwaukee band leader Paul Cebar credits his early Summerfest experiences as a teenage fan with helping steer him toward a music career.

"I remember the day that Carlin was arrested," he says. "That whole day was tremendous.

"That was the (year of the) Doors without Jim. Jim had

Buddy Montgomery was featured at the Miller Jazz Oasis on July 11, 1975.

MILWAUKEE WORLD FESTIVAL INC.

JOURNAL SENTINEL

Neal Schon of Journey tuned up backstage July 5, 1978.

died. It was actually great. They were great. I loved them. Dr. John was there that day, and he was in full regalia, the full deal, the feathers and everything. It was tremendous, and that was quite influential in my development. I loved him. I was really, like, 'Whoa. What is that?'

"I remember very well Ella Fitzgerald. I was down there in the fog. I remember it being one of those chilly nights. I remember as a very young guy, my folks took me down to see (Duke) Ellington. I remember he had just a weird little ponytail. . . . I remember the look of it more than I remember the sound of it.

"Sonny Rollins. Man, two nights of him. I remember that being stupendous. That was really something else.

"Furry Lewis was called in one night. Sonny Terry and Brownie McGhee were on earlier, and then they brought Furry Lewis in, and he was as drunk as a skunk and about 80. It was very wild. It was another foggy night.

"It was like another world from another time."

Jackson Browne:
main stage
June 30, 1980

Bruce Hornsby & the Range:
Marcus Amphitheater
June 26,1987

JOURNAL SENTINEL

JOURNAL SENTINEL

Spyro Gyra:
Miller Jazz Oasis
June 30,1981

JOURNAL SENTINEL

Emmylou Harris:
main stage
July 5, 1980

Tony Bennett:
main stage
June 26, 1981

JOURNAL SENTINEL

JOURNAL SENTINEL

Kenny Loggins:
main stage
June 28, 1980

JOURNAL SENTINEL

The Moody Blues:
main stage
July 1, 1984

Country singing star Crystal Gayle performed on the main stage with the Milwaukee Symphony Orchestra on July 4, 1985.

MILWAUKEE WORLD FESTIVAL INC.

MILWAUKEE WORLD FESTIVAL INC.

MILWAUKEE WORLD FESTIVAL INC.

Patti LaBelle: main stage July 1, 1986

The Go-Go's: main stage July 5, 1984

MILWAUKEE WORLD FESTIVAL INC.

Asleep at the Wheel (Ray Benson shown): Dance Pavilion, two nights in June 1987

Duran Duran (Simon Le Bon shown): Marcus Amphitheater July 1, 1987

Comedian Dana Carvey: Mix Stage June 28, 1987

MILWAUKEE WORLD FESTIVAL INC.

MILWAUKEE WORLD FESTIVAL INC.

MILWAUKEE WORLD FESTIVAL INC.

Luther Vandross: main stage June 29, 1984

Kenny Chesney's high-energy show headlined the Marcus Amphitheater on July 4, 2006, with Jake Owen opening.

Musical memories

**Donna Summer:
main stage
July 5, 1983**

With so much music swirling through the grounds over four decades, it's no wonder that so many conversations about Summerfest start with "Do you remember seeing. . . ?" or "What year was it that. . .?" In the course of striving for both diversity and mass appeal, the festival has managed to touch most of the major bases of contemporary music.

It certainly isn't a classical music event, but the Milwaukee Symphony Orchestra, often paired with a jazz or pop star, was a featured act for many years. It's not a country music celebration, but it has played host to down-home superstars from Johnny Cash and Willie Nelson to Kenny Chesney and Shania Twain. It's not a rock festival, but much of the membership of the Rock and Roll Hall of Fame has stopped by. Many of the giants of urban music, from James Brown and Aretha Franklin to Alicia Keys and Lauryn

Hill, have paid a visit.

In fact, most of the major music figures of the second half of the 20th century have played Summerfest, often more than once.

Whenever there was a musical change of season, Summerfest kept pace. When outlaw country took off in the '70s, the smiley face shone upon Willie and Waylon. When southern rock was in vogue, the Allman Brothers, Charlie Daniels and Wet Willie came to the lakefront. When the early '90s zydeco boom made accordions all the rage, Summerfest kept up with Buckwheat Zydeco, Terrance Simien, C.J. Chenier and Wayne Toups.

When disco fever was rampant, the festival welcomed Kool & the Gang, Donna Summer and Shalamar. In the '90s swing came back into fashion, and Summerfest answered with Cherry Poppin' Daddies, the Brian Setzer Orchestra and the Phil Collins Big Band. When kiddie queens were in fashion,

Britney Spears, Christina Aguilera and Jessica Simpson played the amphitheater.

Lesley Gore sang some of her 11 top 40 pop hits from the mid-'60s on the Briggs & Stratton stage on June 29, 2000.

The Allman Brothers Band (Gregg Allman shown): Marcus Amphitheater June 30, 2000

Kenneth Schermerhorn led the Milwaukee Symphony Orchestra in a July 4, 1982, performance on the main stage. The MSO played there or at the Marcus almost every year in the 1970s and '80s, and less often in the '90s. The last time was in 2000.

When folk **rocked**

Family friendly but hip enough for hippies, folk music was a staple in the early days of Summerfest. Among the acts to play the festival in the '70s were Melanie, Harry Chapin, Joan Baez, Mary Travers, John Hartford, Ramblin' Jack Elliott, Judy Collins, Steve Goodman, John Prine, Tom Paxton, Doc Watson, Josh White Jr., the Kingston Trio and Gordon Lightfoot.

None of them, though, topped two generations of folk music royalty who made repeat visits to the main stage in the late '70s and early '80s. Describing the 1980 appearance of Pete Seeger and Arlo Guthrie, the Sentinel wrote: "Like a lake breeze blowing a bit of cinder in the eye of the establishment, the pair wasted no time in attacking lies, deflating corporate egos and roasting sacred cows. . . . Guthrie's gentle humor was obvious in a parody of mail-or-

Pete Seeger (right) and Arlo Guthrie sang their folk tunes on the main stage on July 3, 1982.

Peter, Paul and Mary harmonized on the main stage June 27, 1981.

der guitar lessons called 'The Arlo Guthrie Supplementary Guitar Tuning Course,' and during his animal stories, 'Groundhog' and 'Me and My Goose,' about a pet that came to supper."

Rowdy country acts from Hank Williams Jr. and the Kentucky Headhunters to Big & Rich and Brooks & Dunn have been long-time Summerfest staples. But the '70s were particularly notable for the rise of the outlaw movement in country music, blending long hair and rock 'n' roll attitude with the populist instincts of traditional country. Most of the shaggier denizens of Dixie made a stop at the lakefront, including Tompall Glaser, Asleep at the Wheel and Jerry Jeff Walker.

Easily the two biggest figures in the move-

ment were the hippie cowpoke Willie Nelson and old "Waymore" — Waylon Jennings. Both of them were regular visitors to Summerfest.

The Journal caught the spirit of the Red Headed Stranger's following at a 1977 main stage show: "Willie Nelson is the godfather of the most bizarre cult that anyone ever thought up late at night under a table in a bar. It is redneck rock. . . . Willie and the boys also did the (Redneck) national anthem Saturday afternoon. It is the lovely 'Up Against the Wall, Redneck Mother.' Befitting a national anthem, the crowd stood and screamed respectfully."

A year earlier, the Journal described the dramatic change in Jennings' image: "There was a time when Jennings was a fairly standard country act. In those days, his hair was slicked back with Wildroot, and he was covered with approximately as much black leather as a La-Z-Boy reclining chair. But to-day he has long, flowing hair that blows in the wind, a bunch of guys with rags around their heads for a backup band and the kind of huge young following that usually only turns out for the musical equivalent of a nuclear power plant explosion."

There are certain risks and unforeseen adventures that go along with booking musical outlaws. Paul Cebar recalls spending an eventful day in 1982 shepherding Texas singer-guitarist Joe Ely around the festival grounds.

"I was a big fan," Cebar says. "I had met him through some friends, so I kind of offered to be his tour guide, me and a friend from Minneapolis who's another musician. . . Apparently his band had already trashed the trailer, which we didn't know. . .

"We kind of hung with Joe, and we ended up over at Carl Perkins' (show). Joe's spitting beer out at Carl, . . . Carl's laughing his head off, laughing like crazy, and then the security guys grabbed Ely. . . by the shoulders and started taking him in the back. Carl stops playing and says, 'That's my friend! Leave him alone!'

"Eventually I had to roll back there. I had played there recently, and the guys knew me. I had to say, 'Hey, man. That's Joe. He just played on the main stage, and he's here and he's a friend of Carl's.' Then he ended up up there (on stage), and he played with him. Then we ended up going to bars. He's trying to play pool. I remember at one point he ended up bull fighting right out here on 8th and Wisconsin. He's a funny dude and sweet as hell."

John Prine:
Old Style Country Stage
June 27, 1985

Musical traditions

Indiana rocker John Mellencamp acknowledged the applause of the audience during his sold-out concert at the Marcus Amphitheater on June 30, 2005.

Old-fashioned rock 'n' roll and R&B have always been a part of the Summerfest mix.

Huey Lewis & the News project the flavor of an R&B bar band, and maybe it's that regular-guy élan that has helped make them such a perennial favorite at Summerfest. Their 1984 show drew one of the biggest crowds to date.

"Thanks to a huge, shrieking Summerfest main stage audience, Huey Lewis and the News celebrated the greatest day in the history of the band in style," wrote the Sentinel.

"Why has the band been so successful? MTV has helped sell them, but the majority of the credit must go to the band's tunes, which are straightforward, likable and hook-filled. Lewis is also a sharp and entertaining frontman who knows how to work a crowd. Performing most of the concert in a sleeveless T-shirt didn't diminish his appeal."

Maybe it's the Midwestern thing. Maybe it's summer music. But artists with a heartland rock 'n' roll style have always done well at Summerfest. Tom Petty is among the most

**Roy Orbison:
Pabst Festival Stage
two nights in June 1986**

frequent guests at the Marcus Amphitheater. The Jayhawks, John Fogerty, Dave Alvin and John Hiatt have all done good business at the festival.

John Mellencamp's socially conscious brand of small-town Indiana rock 'n' roll has proved a popular fit for Summerfest over three decades. The Journal wrote of a 1988 show: "There is a strange appeal in watching a guy hypnotize 23,000 rock fans with songs about racism, poverty and bank foreclosures."

Oldies are another tradition at Summerfest. For many years, the Pabst Festival Stage was a dependable showcase for rock 'n' roll pioneers such as Chubby Checker, Jerry Lee Lewis, Rick Nelson, Fats Domino, Dion and Roy Orbison.

In fact, Orbison played the Pabst stage in 1984, a few years before he began his 11th-hour comeback with the Traveling Wilburys and as a solo act. Years later, now-retired Pabst stage manager Bob Milkovich remembers that Orbison played that entire show while passing a kidney stone.

Whatever pain he was in was clearly not evident. The Journal wrote that the singer's

John Fogerty (left) and John Mellencamp congratulated each other after singing together at the Marcus Amphitheater on June 30, 2005. Fogerty opened for Mellencamp and then joined him for a song.

operatic pipes were still in top form: "Orbison on a life-support system would probably still have more range than most rock singers today. Orbison in top voice is nothing short of a marvel, and he was in his best form at Summerfest.

"He wavered ever so slightly during the early notes of his first number, 'Only the Lonely'; then it happened — the magic high note in the middle of the song. The crowd of 9,000 whooped, and Orbison took off."

Chubby Checker twisted his way onto many Summerfest stages over the years.

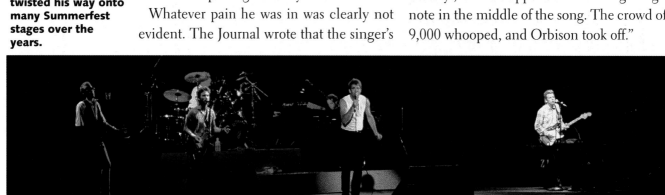

Huey Lewis & the News still had their big hit "The Heart of Rock & Roll" riding high on the charts when they played the main stage on July 8, 1984. Three weeks later, their followup, "If This Is It," would hit the pop charts and crack the top 10.

We saw them when . . .

One of the long-term joys of Summerfest has been seeing acts on their way up — and sometimes, on their way back down. You can read the trajectory of a career in Summerfest bookings. Jay Leno, Billy Crystal, Lewis Black and Dave Chappelle are just a few of the stand-ups who played the comedy stage as they were building into major stars.

Tina Turner electrified the Pabst Festival Stage audiences for two amazing nights in 1983, one year before her big comeback as a solo artist.

Sting performed on the Marcus Amphitheater stage July 10, 1988.

Long before "Thriller," Michael Jackson played Summerfest — in 1971 with the Jackson 5. Long before the Parrothead Nation of fans came to be, Jimmy Buffett was a grounds-stage act playing the Schlitz Country stage in 1975. R.E.M. and the Violent Femmes both played the rock stage in 1983, the year their debut albums were released, and before they began their ascent to the forefront of the '80s rock scene.

Also in 1983, Summerfest's "oldies" Pabst stage caught a true legend on the cusp of what might be rock's greatest comeback.

After breaking up with husband Ike Turner and briefly being on food stamps, Tina Turner came roaring out of nowhere the summer before the release of her phenomenal 1984 comeback album, "Private Dancer." For two nights Turner, then in her mid-40s, wowed the Pabst stage audience.

Run-DMC brought rap to the Marcus Amphitheater on June 30, 1987.

Gwen Stefani, singer for No Doubt, ran across the Marcus stage during an energetic performance on July 2, 1997.

"She made sure that everyone who saw her that night would remember her forever," the Journal recalled in 1987. "Turner exploded into view in a thigh-high shredded-leather dress, shimmying through 'Putting Out Fire' and 'Hot Legs.' She left the crowd drained but exultant an hour later. Still, few fans even then imagined they had witnessed one of the first steps in Turner's amazing comeback journey and that the remarkable 'Private Dancer' album was just around the corner."

Then-Pabst stage manager Milkovich remembers getting her for bargain prices, and that off-stage Turner was anything but the commanding tigress people saw in performance.

"I've never, of all the entertainers I've seen, seen a more nervous entertainer than Tina Turner before she went on stage. She was literally shaking. Her manager was standing in front of her, he was holding her hands. She was literally shaking.

"I remember paying her $15,000 for two days. Two one-hour shows. The following year (entertainment director Bob) Babisch tried to book her. She wanted $150,000 with a $5,000 personal rider."

Jimmy Buffett:
main stage
July 1, 1985

Adam Duritz, lead singer of Counting Crows, got signs of approval from fans who lined the stage during the July 3, 1997, performance at the Marcus.

JOURNAL SENTINEL

Brian McKnight performed at the Marcus Amphitheater in support of Mary J. Blige on July 1, 1998.

JOURNAL SENTINEL

JOURNAL SENTINEL

LeAnn Rimes accepted flowers from a fan on June 30, 1998, at the Marcus Amphitheater.

JOURNAL SENTINEL

Dave Schools of headliner Widespread Panic bellows at the microphone during the band's July 2 1998, show at the Marcus Amphi theater.

JOURNAL SENTINEL

Meat Loaf didn't need anyone to open for him on the Marcus stage July 2, 1996.

Alan Jackson:
Marcus Amphitheater
June 29, 1999

Dave Matthews:
Marcus Amphitheater
June 28, 1999

JOURNAL SENTINEL

New Edition:
Marcus
Amphitheater
July 1, 1997

JOURNAL SENTINEL

JOURNAL SENTINEL

JOURNAL SENTINEL

Bonnie Raitt:
Marcus Amphitheater
June 29, 1998

James Taylor:
Marcus Amphitheater
July 6, 1997

JOURNAL SENTINEL

Phil Collins Big Band:
Marcus Amphitheater
June 26, 1998

Bluesmen **and divas**

Eric Clapton closed the main stage lineup for 1983 with some English blues.

MILWAUKEE WORLD FESTIVAL INC.

Maybe it's the proximity to Chicago, but the blues have also been a Summerfest staple. B.B. King was one of the biggest names to play the second Summerfest in 1969. Over the years, most of the great blues legends have paid a visit to the lakefront, including John Lee Hooker, Buddy Guy, Albert King, Johnny Winter, Koko Taylor, Willie Dixon, Luther Allison, Junior Wells, Charles Brown and Ruth Brown.

MILWAUKEE WORLD FESTIVAL INC.

Stevie Ray Vaughan preached his blues three times at Summerfest before his death in 1990. His only main stage appearance was on July 2, 1986 (shown). His previous two performances, in 1983 and '84, were on the rock stage.

The Journal wrote of a twilight performance by a still-formidable Muddy Waters in 1981, two years before his death: "All the old-time riffs were there, as round and perfect as the day they first came out of his guitar. And as for his singing, Waters can still pack more feeling into one 'oh, baby' than most modern blues singers can wring from an entire set."

If you had to pick one musician who has most influenced the sound of modern Summerfest, it might well be the late Stevie Ray Vaughan. The Texas legend died in a helicopter crash near Alpine Valley Music Theatre in East Troy in 1990, but his muscular

Whitney Houston was already a big star when she performed at the Marcus Amphitheater on July 5, 1987. She had the megahit "I Wanna Dance With Somebody (Who Loves Me)" high in the charts, the fourth in a streak of seven chart-topping singles in a row.

**Stevie Nicks:
Marcus Amphitheater
July 4, 2005**

style of blues rock can still be heard around the festival grounds at all hours, and the originator himself played the rock stage in 1983 and '84 before moving up to the main stage in 1986.

"With one solo, Stevie Ray Vaughan says more than others do in an hour . . .," the Journal wrote of the '86 show. "From the show-opening instrumental barrage of 'Scuttle Buttin' ' and 'Soul to Soul' to the amphetamine boogie assault of the encore 'Love Struck Baby,' Vaughan made gutsy, unpredictable blues-rock playing seem pathetically easy."

Most of the great men of soul have played Summerfest, too: Ray Charles, Smokey Robinson, James Brown, Freddie Jackson, Luther Vandross and Wilson Pickett among them. Summerfest's Vic Thomas remembers the time his sister was overwhelmed by the star power of Teddy Pendergrass in 1980

"At the time he was the hottest of the hottest," Thomas recalls. "I still remember my sister being backstage, and he walked up and waved to her and she fainted. She just couldn't believe that Teddy Pendergrass waved to her."

Many of the great R&B divas have made a Summerfest stop or two: Anita Baker, Patti Labelle, Mary J. Blige, Whitney Houston

Teddy Pendergrass brought his sexy soul appeal to the main stage on June 27, 1980. Less than two years later, a traffic accident would leave him paralyzed from the neck down.

Cher performed in a black and flesh-toned outfit at the Marcus Amphitheater, July 6,1990.

**Mary J. Blige:
Marcus Amphitheater
July 3, 2006**

Anita Baker (left) kicked up her heels as she performed at the Marcus Amphitheater on July 3, 1990.

and Gladys Knight, among others. And, of course, the greatest of them all: Lady Soul herself.

"Aretha Franklin, with the intermittent support of the Milwaukee Symphony Orchestra, took over Summerfest's Marcus Amphitheater Friday night and drew a crowd that Dwight Yoakam would have given up his skin-tight leather pants for," the Journal Sentinel wrote in 1996. "At 54, the Queen of Soul is truly queen-sized, but the energy, the pipes and the interest all still seem to be

there."

Janet Jackson was riding at the top of the urban music and pop scene in 1994 when the Journal described the lavish spectacle of her amphitheater concert:

"There was the usual whiz-bang stuff: hydraulic platforms, multiple costume changes, five video screens, and sparks and flames and fireworks galore. But the most impressive sight was that of Jackson and her eight dancers whizzing across the stage in sync like whirling dervishes.

"They sweat buckets as they danced around in the humid, 85-degree heat. But Jackson and her crew of six women and two men refused to let a little muggy weather make them wilt. They blazed through the flashy medieval carnival routine of 'When I Think of You'/ 'Escapade'/ 'Miss You Much'; re-created the 1940s in colorful zoot suits during 'Alright' and marched with conviction through the mock military routines of 'Rhythm Nation.' "

The Foo Fighters (lead guitarist Dave Grohl shown) played to a sold-out crowd at the Marcus Amphitheater on July 2, 2000. The Red Hot Chili Peppers headlined the show.

Lynyrd Skynyrd lead singer Johnny Van Zant entertained the crowd with a high-energy performance at the Marcus on July 3, 1999

JOURNAL SENTINEL

JOURNAL SENTII

JOURNAL SENTINEL

Sheryl Crow kicked off Summerfest 2002's Marcus Amphitheater performances with her June 27 set.

Rockin' at the 'Fest

Although Summerfest swore off hard rock after a rowdy crowd scene at the 1973 Humble Pie concert, the festival eventually relented. Following an inauspicious 1971 debut in the flea market area, the rock stage became a permanent part of the lineup in 1973, and in the years since then much of the hard rock, grunge and metal community has rattled the rafters.

The main stage roster has included Tesla, Poison, Pearl Jam, Warrant, the Red Hot Chili Peppers, Soundgarden, Def Leppard and Nine Inch Nails. In 1992 and 1994, one of metal's most enduring institutions, Metallica, played the amphitheater.

"Friday was blunt-force trauma night at Summerfest, a double whack upside the horns called Metallica," the Sentinel wrote of the 1994 show. "The most sought-after ticket at Summerfest, Metallica is an interesting anomaly, a band that's become a major commercial force by refusing to do any of the usual commercial things.

"No sensitive power ballads from Metallica.

The Dead performed at the Marcus Amphitheater on July 1, 2003. Shown are (from left) Joan Osborne, Bob Weir and a band member's daughter, who wandered onto the stage.

MILWAUKEE WORLD FESTIVAL INC.

JOURNAL SENTINEL

JOURNAL SENTINEL

Mick Fleetwood was surrounded by percussion instruments as Fleetwood Mac performed before a sold-out crowd at the Marcus Amphitheater on June 29, 2003. The show featured the band's near-classic lineup: Fleetwood on drums, singer Stevie Nicks, singer-guitarist Lindsay Buckingham and bassist John McVie.

the festival were male. In the early '90s, Alanis Morissette's debut album "Jagged Little Pill" introduced a new kind of pop princess: angry, profane, sexually direct and even a bit neurotic. In 1996, the Journal Sentinel wrote: "What distinguishes Morissette — besides vocal cords that seem to have been hotwired directly to her central nervous system — is that she makes driven, uncompromising hard rock out of the kind of internal subject matter that's usually relegated to jangly folk ballads or polite pop music."

And while the instincts of Summerfest have always been focused on the mainstream, that doesn't mean the festival hasn't been willing to host some of the more controversial figures of the music world. As the Journal Sentinel recounted, R. Kelly didn't modify the salacious qualities of his stage show for a Summerfest audience in 1996: " 'Hump Bounce,' the opening number, pretty well set the tone for a night where the most burning question was whether Kelly would take off his pants. He did debrief, briefly."

No pretty frontmen, not even a keyboard. It's just three guitars, a drummer and good old knock-your-molars-out rock 'n' roll. . . .We saw one fan at the sold-out concert choking his buddy. This is indeed music as combat."

Not all the aggression-laden acts to play

As Summerfest — along with popular music itself — matured into a more sophisticated, professionally run business, there were fewer tense incidents along the lines of Sly and Humble Pie. But when you're dealing with musicians, divas and other temperamental talents, there are still plenty of nerve-wracking moments.

Royalty has its prerogatives, as His Royal Badness proved by testing the patience of his fans, Sly-style, at his 2004 Summerfest show.

As the Journal Sentinel recounted: "Prince kept an eager crowd of about 21,000 waiting two hours past the start time printed on their tickets Thursday evening at the Marcus Amphitheater. But the man who has innovated his own sound, a flawless meld of funk, rock, pop and whatever else strikes his fancy, has surely earned the right to operate in his own time zone.

"His trademark spins and orgiastic guitar solos are still as sharp as the cut of his clothes, but Thursday night he also showed a warmth and intimacy that was sometimes lacking during the '90s, when musical experimentation and a bitter feud with his former label seemed to take center stage. Pulling a young audience member on stage during a free-form jam, Prince gave his sly smile and quipped, 'Don't fall, sugar. I ain't got no insurance.' "

Another artist who rattled the nerves of Summerfest management was the late, great Ray Charles. In 2002 he was booked to play the Briggs & Stratton Big Backyard, but the afternoon of the gig, entertainment director Bob Babisch got a call from Charles' road manager telling him he couldn't do the show.

JOURNAL SENTINEL

R. Kelly: Marcus Amphitheater, June 27, 1999

Backstage stories

Prince entertained the crowd at the Marcus Amphitheater to open Summerfest on June 28, 2001.

Why not, Babisch asked.

The manager explained that as a blind person, Charles had heightened sensitivity to ambient noise, and all the sound from the surrounding stages and the midway meant Charles couldn't possibly play the festival. The distraction would be overwhelming.

Babisch was desperate. It was too late to get another headliner. He ordered the midway shut down and told the nearby Harley-Davidson Roadhouse to hold off the start time for its headliner, rising country star Keith Urban. Charles showed up to an uncharacteristically quiet Big Backyard, but he was slow going on, and his band played a warm-up set. Meanwhile, the crowd at the Harley stage was starting to chant for Urban. Finally, Urban went on just as Charles was starting up.

The upshot: After all the work to create a quiet stage, Charles ended up playing his set while thousands of female fans screamed for Urban just a few hundred feet away — and if Charles was bothered by the noise, he never gave any indication.

Musicians sometimes act in mysterious ways. Summerfest's Vic Thomas remembers that when the Beach Boys got to the festival one year, drummer Dennis Wilson jumped into Lake Michigan for what must have been a bracing swim.

Not every celebrity likes to make such a splashy entrance. Bob Milkovich remembers one headliner who literally dropped in on the Pabst stage.

As is customary, Milkovich had sent a limo to the airport to pick up his headliner.

"I got a call from the limo driver. He says, 'I've been waiting for a half-hour, nothing. . .' All of a sudden at the back of the old Pabst stage, four security guys jump this guy because he jumped over the fence. It was Weird Al (Yankovic). He says, 'I'm Weird Al! I've got to talk to Bob Milkovich!' They're holding him, and I say, 'Where the hell were you?'

" 'Oh,' he says, 'I like to come in incognito.' "

With its many different stages, Summerfest is naturally set up for musicians to visit one another.

Vic Thomas recalls: "I remember if you booked Elvin Bishop, it seemed you got five shows out of him because he'd play on the main stage and then go to every other stage and jam with whoever was there. He jammed with Spyro Gyra. He jammed with Muddy Waters. That's the kind of musician he was."

Sometimes those backstage meetings are arranged with the secrecy of an international summit. Milkovich remembers one especially celebrated guest who came to pay Johnny Rivers a visit at the old Pabst stage in 1989. It started with a mysterious call from Security Director John Rutley.

"He says to me, 'There's a special guest coming to your stage.'

"I said, 'Well, who is it?'

"He says, 'I can't tell you.'

"I say, 'Wait a minute. You want to come to my back stage, and you won't tell me who it is? No goddamn way. I want to know who it is.'

"He wouldn't tell me. I finally gave in. All of a sudden there's, like, 15 security guards. This guy is in between them. He's got a hood over his head. You can't see who it is. It's like one of those people from 'Star Wars.' It was Dylan, and he came to see Johnny Rivers."

Vic Thomas adds a funny note about the story. All Dylan had said after his amphitheater show was that he wanted to see "Johnny," so Summerfest security took him backstage at the old Old Style Stage, where Johnny Winter was playing.

"We were all expecting one of those great history-making moments where Johnny Winter would jam with Bob Dylan," Thomas recalls. "They came within eyeshot of each other, and Dylan said, 'Where's Johnny Rivers?' " Taken aback, Dylan's entourage hustled him through the grounds, on foot, to the Pabst stage where, Thomas recalls, Dylan was "overjoyed" to see Rivers.

Dylan played Summerfest one other time, with Paul Simon at the amphitheater in 1999. If he visited any other performers that year, no one's talking.

JOURNAL SENTINEL

Warren Haynes played with the Allman Brothers at the Marcus Amphitheater on July 5, 2005. When he was at Summerfest on June 28, 2002, he played three shows that day with three different bands: The Allman Brothers and Phil Lesh & Friends on the Marcus stage and with Gov't Mule on a grounds stage.

Frank Black of the Pixies:
Marcus Amphitheater
July 7, 2005

Smashing Pumpkins'
lead singer Billy Corgan:
Marcus Amphitheater
July 5, 1998

D' Angelo:
Marcus Amphitheater
July 4, 2000

Trent Reznor o
Nine Inch Nails
Marcus
Amphitheater
July 2, 2006

Brooks & Dunn
(Kix Brooks, left,
and Ronnie Dunn):
Marcus
Amphitheater
June 29, 2002

Destiny's Child
(Kelly Rowland,
Beyoncé Knowles
and Michelle Wil-
liams, left to right):
Marcus
Amphitheater
July 2, 2001

Alicia Keys:
Marcus
Amphitheater
July 2, 2002

Michael Kang, a member of String Cheese Incident, played at the Marcus Amphitheater on July 6, 2006.

On July 1, 2000, Christina Aguilera opened her Marcus Amphitheater show with her hit, "Genie in a Bottle."

Lead singer Joel Madden of Good Charlotte rocked the Marcus on July 6, 2003.

JOURNAL SENTINEL

JOURNAL SENTINEL

JOURNAL SENTINEL

Elvis Costello performed with the Imposters and Allen Toussaint on June 29, 2006, at the Briggs & Stratton Big Backyard on opening night of Summerfest.

JOURNAL SENTINEL

John Rzeznik (left) and Robby Takac with the Goo Goo Dolls performed at the Marcus on July 9, 2006.

Violent Femmes guitarist Gordan Gano performed at the rock stage on July 2, 1984.

Brian Ritchie of the Violent Femmes goes acoustic during the group's appearance on the main stage on June 27, 1986.

Hometown heroes

Seeing bands at Summerfest undoubtedly inspired many area teens to pursue their dream of a career in music.

Local acts have always been a big part of Summerfest, even though the festival can be a mixed bag for them: They get the exposure of playing a prestigious event, but they're often relegated to daytime slots when fewer people see them. Even so, many hometown favorites have become synonymous with Summerfest: Eddie Butts, the Booze Brothers, Deluxury, the Love Monkeys, Sigmund Snopek III and Pat McCurdy, to name just a few.

Probably no bands have had a longer or more mutually profitable association with Summerfest than the BoDeans and the Violent Femmes.

**Jerry Harrison:
Marcus Amphitheater, July 1, 1990**

The Femmes are recognized as punk pioneers, and they've toured all over the world, but drummer Victor DeLorenzo says playing for the home folks was always one of their biggest kicks.

"I think one of the first times we played was the rock stage. . . . That must have been maybe '83. Obviously, living in Milwaukee, I had been going to Summerfest for years. For me and for the band, it was such a big thrill to not only play something that was a legitimate venue but also be able to play in front of all of our friends.

"We just had a great turnout, and it was one of the few places we could play in the world where we could command that many audience members at a single show. In other parts of the world we were still in the club or smaller - theater part of our career. . .

"I would have to say unequivocally that Summerfest has been very, very good for us."

Milwaukee native Eric Benet performed at the Marcus Amphitheater on July 4, 2000.

From the late '80s onward, the BoDeans have been a regular presence at Summerfest, where they play to enthusiastic and packed crowds. At Summerfest, people like Warren Zevon, Roger McGuinn and Chris Isaak are just opening acts for the BoDeans.

The Journal Sentinel described the scene in 2004 when two hometown heroes, Steve

Milwaukee musician Sigmund Snopek III, shown performing at Summerfest in 1984, has been a perennial presence at the festival.

Miller and the BoDeans, played a co-head-lining show:

"If you're a BoDean, Summerfest is like Christmas, New Year's, Fourth of July and your birthday rolled into one. For one night a year, an aging club band with one minor hit becomes a legitimate amphitheater act playing before an adoring crowd that sings along with every chorus and stays on its feet.

"When Sam Llanas said, 'Milwaukee, there's no place like home,' he surely meant it."

Singer-guitarist Llanas recently reflected on what those amphitheater homecomings meant to him:

"The Marcus experience is a surreal ex-perience. You're standing on a stage where there's 20,000-plus people out there. It's hard to take it all in.

"A few times there have been some beau-tiful thunderstorms, so the lightning would come in and it would light up the whole crowd. One year, it must have been the best light show ever.

"Two years ago, I think we realized that might be the last time we were going to be playing the Marcus. So I just took a few min-utes to take it all in.

"I really appreciate that experience. It's hard because you are working, but it's nice just to take a few moments for yourself and enjoy it."

The BoDeans' Kurt Neu-mann (left) and Sam Llanas played new material on the Marcus Amphitheater stage on July 3, 2003.

MILWAUKEE WORLD FESTIVAL INC.

the future

As it celebrates its 40th birthday, Summerfest has moved far beyond the issues of mere survival that defined its early years.

Today it is a secure, well-established event recognized nationally and even internationally as one of the nation's leading festivals.

"Music festivals come and go across the country," says Don Smiley, who has been at the Summerfest helm since 2004. "Summerfest has done a remarkable job in sustaining itself for 40 years. It really and truly is special when you think about that."

But even mature events face challenges. Today, more than ever, Summerfest is a bratwurst-budget event in a filet-mignon music business. In the years ahead it will have to find ways to keep pace with the rising costs of big-name entertainment while still honoring Mayor Henry Maier's mission to remain accessible and affordable to the average Milwaukeean.

Smiley says he believes the festival will have to treat the amphitheater shows and the rest of the festival as separate entities. The grounds stages would continue to offer name entertainment at bargain prices, while the amphitheater shows would reflect the economic realities of booking some of the top acts in popular music.

More than ever, Summerfest also is under pressure to present an attractive, aesthetically pleasing site. When it was surrounded by fields and fans were up to their ankles in mud, any kind of solid surface underfoot was an improvement. Now Summerfest has to compete visually with upscale new neighbors such as the Milwaukee Art Museum's Calatrava addition, Pier Wisconsin, a new state park and the revitalized Third Ward.

Construction of the new $3 million Miller Lite Oasis in 2006 was a vivid example of the kind of work that needs to be done. With an expanded viewing area, improved traffic flow and projection TV screens, the Oasis has set a new standard for the festival's grounds stages. The next step, Smiley says, is a new south gate and improvements to the south end of the grounds near the Marcus Amphitheater.

Chicagoans Tony Margando and Patti Schiefelbein relaxed in the shade along the lakefront at Summerfest on July 4, 1985.

Previous page: Children played in the new cooling fountains at Summerfest on opening day in 2002.

Pat McCurdy played on the Potawatomi Classic Rock Stage on July 1, 2005.

Tom Doyle and his daughter, Kelly, 5, didn't let rain dampen their fun at the Harley-Davidson Roadhouse during a performance by the Jack Grassel Band on June 30, 1997.

But just thinking about where Summerfest is going, you can't help but remember where it's been and the impression it has made on so many people — especially the musicians who went as kids and are now creating memories for a whole new generation of fans:

Pat McCurdy:

"I don't think I was even 10 years old, and I went to see Chicago in the middle of a rainy field.... You're 10 years old and an aspiring guitar player, and the guy starts the solo from '25 or 6 to 4.' It was exciting, and I hadn't been to many shows....

"The first time I played there I was maybe 21 or 22. Even then it was a big, big show. There's no doubt about that. I still get that sense, and I've done it a trillion times....

"What else is that big or classy anywhere around here? We're surrounded by cities with way more money and way more population, but they still can't muster something that nice."

Connie Grauer, of Mrs. Fun:

"I lived in Waukesha, so my parents weren't that hot on me going (to Summerfest).... I had to wait until I got my license....

"As a 16-year-old driving in there, it was the most wonderful thing.... I'd started playing (gigs) when I was 13, so I was totally into it.... I couldn't wait to get there. I spent all day, as long as I could until I had to leave to go home, which was about 8 o'clock at night."

Some couples even get married at Summerfest, including Shannon Werner and Brian Grant, both of Milwaukee, at the Ticketmaster Legends stage on July 1, 2000.

Jane Martin and Bob Leitinger, of Milwaukee, found a quiet spot near the Marcus Amphitheater to steal a kiss at the end of a day together at Summerfest in 1987.

John Hauser, of the Love Monkeys:

"My first Summerfest was watching the Jackson 5. ... I was 10. ... My brothers took me. It was probably my first concert without my parents when I was a little kid. ... The stage was just out in the open. There weren't many places to sit. It was more of a big field. I remember kids sitting on top of trailers singing songs. ... It was a wonderful experience. ...

"I think it's the ultimate band gig for anybody in Milwaukee. Summerfest is just a staple of a Milwaukee summer. ... We were together for four years before we got a Summerfest show, so we had to deal with three or four years of people asking, 'Are you playing Summerfest?' I think the beautiful thing for us was, it was our fifth year of being together (when) we finally played Summerfest, and we were ready.

"When you're a kid and you play Summerfest for the first time, in your eyes, you've made it, whether you ever do anything else for the rest of your life."

the headliners

Summerfest headliners from 1968 through 2006

1968

Pre–summerfest activities

Miller 200 mile stock car race; performances by Rick Nelson, Roy Clark, ventriloquist Jimmy Nelson (State Fair Park)

Music Under the Stars (Milwaukee County Parks)

Greater Milwaukee Open (North Shore Country Club)

National lawn bowling tournament (Lake Park)

National clay court tennis tournament (Town Club)

Summerfest activities
July 19-28

Youth Fest (lakefront)

40 youth exhibits, Flying Palacios trapeze act, Great Zacchini cannon act, "Syncopated Waters"

The Robbs (17 shows)

The Destinations

The New Colony Six (four shows)

The Messengers

Freddy Cannon

Ronnie Dove (six shows)

The Esquires

The Secrets

The Picture

The Lemon Pipers

The Next Five

Also at the lakefront: water ski shows, fireworks, boat race, parachute jumps, speed shift carousel by American Motors

Other locations (highlights)

Up With People (County Stadium)

Royal Philharmonic of London (Blatz Temple of Music, Washington Park)

The National Ballet of Mexico; National Polka Festival (Auditorium)

Gerhard Rudolph's band (Pere Marquette Park)

Miss Milwaukee Pageant; Wisconsin Idea Theater (MATC)

International Folk Festival (Arena)

Gooding's Million Dollar midway (N. Cass and E. Clybourn streets)

"White Lightning" sculpture-in-light show (Memorial Center)

International Film Festival (Palace Theater)

Wisconsin Spectacle of Music (downtown parade)

Greek carnival (Annunciation Greek Orthodox Church)

"Around the World in 80 Minutes" (Washington Park)

The "Spirit of Youth Negro achievement show"; "Houdini" magic show (Civic Plaza)

Indian lore exhibits, films, dances (Milwaukee Museum)

Air Age '68 (General Mitchell Field)

"Salute to Milwaukee" dinner (Pfister Hotel)

Special events and seminars for women (Cardinal Stritch University, Mount Mary College, Alverno College)

1969

Pre-summerfest activities

Miller 200-mile stock car race; performance by Vikki Carr (State Fair Park)

Water ski shows (lakefront)

Milwaukee Sentinel golf tournaments

Polo (Uihlein field)

Summerfest activities
July 18-27

Youth Fest (lakefront)

The Lemon Pipers

Bob Seger System/Soup

The Box Tops/The Wrest/Freddie and the Freeloaders

Crazy Elephant

Ohio Express/Unchained Mynds/Matt King

Brooklyn Bridge/1910 Fruitgum Company

University Blues Band

Peppermint Rainbow

The American Band

Also at the lakefront: Flying Indians of Acapulco; International Picnicfest; Venetian boat parade; "Spirit of Youth '69"

Other locations (highlights)

Bob Hope (County Stadium, two shows)

B.B. King/The Staple Singers/Wilson Pickett/William Bell (Arena)

Opera Associates of Milwaukee (University of Wisconsin-Milwaukee)

** Performer and event information was provided by Summerfest and supplemented by Milwaukee Journal Sentinel archives. Due to unrecorded schedule changes and cancellations, some performers may not have appeared as listed. Each stage's acts are listed generally in order from opening day to closing day. Some of the smaller stages are not included here.

The Irish Freedom folk singers (Memorial Center)
Gerald Rudolph German band (Zeidler Park)
Ahmad Jamal Jazz Trio (Arena)
Ferrante & Teicher (Washington Park)
Porter Wagoner/Dolly Parton/Tex Ritter (Arena)
Military Band Concert (County Stadium)
St. Lewis Opera Company (Washington Park)
National Ballet of Mexico (Arena)
Ramsey Lewis Trio (UWM Ballroom)
Ralph Herman Orchestra, jazz and Dixieland bands, San Francisco Musical Arts Ensemble, "Night in Bavaria" (Civic Center Plaza)
Milwaukee Musicfest talent competitions (Sheraton-Schroeder Hotel)
National Polka Festival (Auditorium)
Air Age '69 (General Mitchell Field)

1970 *July 17-26*

Lakefront Stage

Pat Paulsen/Jose Feliciano
The Cowsills/Earl Scruggs Revue
Chicago/Lorin Hollander
James Brown and Revue/Bare Fat
Rotary Connection/Procol Harum
Bobby Sherman/Andy Kim
Cannonball Adderley/Ramsey Lewis
Sarah Vaughan/Rahsaan Roland Kirk
Doc Severinsen/The Esquires
Sly and the Family Stone/The Wrest

People waiting to get into the 1977 festival got a big greeting from Summerfest.

Other locations

Pierre Boulez and the Cleveland Orchestra (Washington Park)
Milwaukee Symphony Orchestra "Zoomphony" (County Zoo)

1971 *July 16-25*

Main Stage

Jose Feliciano/Judy Collins/David Steinberg/Siegel-Schwall Band
Roy Clark/Ray Price/Jeannie C. Riley/Sonny James
Bobby Sherman/ Milwaukee Symphony/The Messengers
Della Reese/Woody Herman & the World's Greatest Jazz Band
B.B. King/Paul Butterfield Blues Band/Muddy Waters/ Luther Allison
Blood, Sweat & Tears
The Jackson 5/Siegel-Schwall Band
Little Richard/Chuck Berry/Bo Diddley/The Coasters/The Drifters/The Aces
Doc Severinsen/The Association/Brothers & Sisters
Mountain/John Sebastian/Poco

Miller High Life Jazz Oasis

Ruedebusch Memorial Band (two nights)
Buddy Montgomery Septet
World's Greatest Jazz Band
George Pritchett Trio (two nights)
Riverboat Ramblers
Jim Robak Orchestra
Boll Weevil Jazz Band
Sig Millonzi Sextet

Flea Market Rock Area

Pandemonium Shadow Show
Soup
Sammy Lay Blues Revival
Larry Lynne
Omaha/ Woodbine Kind/Neal Gavens/Hound Dog Band
Siegel-Schwall Band
Jerry Blake Orchestra
Stars & Stripes
The Messengers
Family at Max

Jazzman Ramsey Lewis played for an estimated 12,000 people at Summerfest 1970.

JOURNAL SENTINEL

1972 *July 14-23*

Main Stage

Glen Campbell
Dionne Warwick/Ray Charles
David Cassidy/The Messengers
Jose Feliciano/Griffin (WOKY Rocks Spectacular)
The Dovells/Gary U.S. Bonds/The Crystals/Jerry Lee Lewis
  (Bill Haley and the Comets and Fats Domino canceled
  due to illness)
Aretha Franklin
Edgar Winter/J. Geils Band/B.B. King
Arlo Guthrie/George Carlin/Siegel-Schwall Band
Charley Pride/Judy Lynn/Leroy Van Dyke
The Doors (minus Jim Morrison, who died in 1971)/
  Quicksilver/Dr. John the Night Tripper/Mahavishnu
  Orchestra/The Phlorescent Leech & Eddie/Eden Stone

Miller Jazz Oasis

Stan Kenton Orchestra
Al Capone Memorial Jazz Band
Jim Robak Orchestra
Riverboat Ramblers (two nights)
George Pritchett Trio
Buddy Montgomery
Boll Weevils
Buddy De Franco and the Glenn Miller Orchestra
Millonzi Sextet

1973 *July 13-22*

Main Stage

Stephen Stills and Manassas
Steve Miller Band/Siegel-Schwall
Sammy Davis Jr./Johnny Brown/Blinky Williams
The Doobie Brothers/New Riders of the Purple Sage
Blood, Sweat & Tears/Curtis Mayfield
Isaac Hayes Movement/Hot Buttered Soul
Milwaukee Symphony Orchestra with Van Cliburn
Buck Owens/Loretta Lynn
Humble Pie and the Blackberries/Jo Jo Gunne
Sergio Mendes & Brasil '77/Leo Kottke/The Pointer Sisters

Rock Stage

Ruby Jones
Sweetbottom/Ben Sidran
Palmer House
Dynamite Duck
Big Muddy
Dick and Sue Thomas
Monroe Doctrine
Bull Frog Band
Soup
Sigmund Snopek III

Miller Jazz Oasis

Sig Millonzi
Chuck Hedges
Ray Tabs and Penny Goodwin
Lionel Hampton
Buddy Montgomery (two nights)
Duke Ellington
Ramsey Lewis Trio
Al Belletto
George Pritchett

1974 *July 12-21*

Main Stage

Seals & Crofts/Heartsfield
Charley Pride/Ronnie Milsap/The Four Guys
Doc Severinsen/Today's Children
The O'Jays/The Moments/The Delfonics
Milwaukee Symphony with Peter Nero
Melanie/Harry Chapin
Gladys Knight and The Pips/Billy Paul
Sha Na Na/Uncle Vinty
Johnny Cash featuring June Carter Cash, Carl Perkins, the
  Tennessee Three, Larry Gatlin
Helen Reddy/Paul Williams

Rock Stage

Unburst
Apothecary/Cheap Trick
Larry Lynne/Solberg Bros.
John Hiatt
Short Stuff/Mighty Joe Young
Directions/Pistol
The Prodigy Show
Major Arcana
Reyna
Cain

Miller Jazz Oasis

Charlie Byrd/Chase (three nights)
Dukes of Dixieland/Charlie Byrd (two nights)
Mose Allison/Chuck Mangione (three nights)
Ramsey Lewis (two nights)

Schlitz Country

Heartsfield
Country Gazette (two nights)
Red Deacon & the Nashtown Nite Shift
Barbara Fairchild
Monroe Doctrine
Earl Scruggs Revue
The Judy Lynn Show
Tanya Tucker (two nights)

Pabst International Folk Festival

Avala Orchestra (two nights)
Louie Byk Band
Verne Meisner Band (two nights)
Don Fleury Band
Eddie Blazonczyk Band (two nights)
Roger Bright Band
Beograd Orchestra

1975 *July 3-13*

Main Stage

Beach Boys
James Taylor/Phoebe Snow
Johnny Rodriguez/Donna Fargo
Gordon Lightfoot/Mary Travers
Blood, Sweat & Tears/David Clayton-Thomas/Maria
   Muldaur
Earth, Wind & Fire/Donald Byrd and the Blackbyrds
Chuck Berry/LaBelle
Ella Fitzgerald and Roy Eldridge
Joan Baez/Hoyt Axton
Roberta Flack/Stanley Turrentine
Bee Gees

Rock Stage

Bill Camplin
Jeanie Stout/Luther Allison
Renya
Punch
Vixen
Cheap Trick
Bo Conlon
Cain
Atlantic Mine
Euphoria
Chicago Daily Blues

Miller Jazz Oasis

Woody Herman (two nights)
Bobby Blue Band (two nights)
Gato Barbieri (two nights)
Cannonball Adderley (three nights)
Maynard Ferguson (two nights)

Schlitz Country

The Roger McGuinn Band/Cassidy
Jimmy Buffett
Ramblin' Jack Elliott
Sonny Terry and Brownie McGhee
Corky Siegel
Asleep at the Wheel (two nights)
John Hartford
Bill Monroe & the Bluegrass Boys
The Vassar Clements Band
The Dillards (two nights)

Pabst International Festival

Los Changuitos Feos Mariachis (two nights)
Roman Hanes Band
John Hoffman Band
Sonrize Band
Eddie Blazonczyk Band (two nights)
Louie Byk Band
Beograd Orchestra
Louis Bashell Band
Don Fleury Band

Comedy Showcase

David Brenner (two nights)
John Byner (two nights)
Edmonds & Curley (two nights)
Ace Trucking Company (two nights)
Divided We Stand (three nights)

1976 *June 30-July 11*

Main Stage

Tony Bennett with Torri Zito/Frankie Lester & All-Time Big Band
War/Martha Velez
Judy Collins
Elvin Bishop
Helen Reddy
John Sebastian
The Ohio Players
The Spinners
Kris Kristofferson and Rita Coolidge
The Band/Leon Redbone
The Outlaw Music festival featuring Waylon Jennings, Jessie Colter, Tompall Glaser and His Outlaw Band
Bobby Vinton

Rock Stage

Atlantic Mine
Jim Schwall
Evans Cole Christmas and Friends
Short Stuff
Sinbad
Jesse Brady
Crossfire
Zuider Zee
Vixen
Circus
Arousing Polaris
Yancy Derringer

Miller Jazz Oasis

Woody Herman (two nights)
Brecker Brothers (two nights)
New Orleans Heritage Hall Jazz Band (two nights)
Dave Brubeck (two nights)
Maynard Ferguson (two nights)
Les McCann (two nights)

Schlitz Country USA

Eric Weissberg and Deliverance (two nights)
Luther Allison/Koko Taylor/John Hammond
Willie Dixon
Jessy Dixon Singers/Mimi Fariña
Steve Goodman (two nights)
Brewer & Shipley (two nights)
Lester Flatt (two nights)
Firefall

Comedy/Variety Showcase

Billy Crystal (two nights)
Stanley Myron Handelman (two nights)
Henny Youngman (three nights)
Edmonds & Curley

Pabst International Festival

Mariachi Cobre (six nights)
Selo Orchestra
U.S. Navy Steel Band (five nights)

1977 *June 30-July 10*

Main Stage

Steve Miller Band/Firefall
Dick Clark's Rock 'n' Roll Revue: Chuck Berry, Chubby Checker, the Coasters, Bobby Vee, the Shirelles, Bobby Lewis
Arlo Guthrie/Pete Seeger
Joey Heatherton (canceled)
Marilyn McCoo & Billy Davis Jr./The Sylvers
Brick/Bootsy's Rubber Band
Kool & the Gang/The Brothers Johnson
Daryl Hall & John Oates/Atlanta Rhythm Section
America
Willie Nelson/Amazing Rhythm Aces
Elvin Bishop

Peaches Records Rock Stage

Jesse Brady
Joey Dee & the Starliners
Rings
The Britins
The Ramones
Luther Allison
Street Corner Band
American Tears
Crack the Sky
UFO
Judas Priest

Miller Jazz Oasis

Grover Washington Jr. (two nights)
Buddy Rich (three nights)
Ramsey Lewis (two nights)
Brecker Brothers (two nights)
Les McCann (two nights)

Schlitz Country Scene

Tompall Glaser
John Lee Hooker (two nights)
Hank Williams Jr. (two nights)
John Prine (two nights)
Don McLean
Earl Scruggs Revue (two nights)
Vassar Clements

Comedy/Variety Showcase

Jerry Van Dyke (three nights)
Morey Amsterdam (three nights)
Jackie Vernon (three nights)
Philip Proctor and Peter Bergman of Firesign Theater (two nights)

Pabst International Festival

Irish Minstrels (three nights)
Tripoli Steel Band - Trinidad (six nights)
Mor Thiam Drums of Fire Music and Dances of Senegal (two nights)

1978 *June 28-July 9*

Main Stage

Boz Scaggs/Little River Band
The Bar-Kays/Cameo
Dolly Parton
Bobby Vinton
Grateful Dead (canceled due to storm)
Marshall Tucker Band
Helen Reddy
Journey/The Hounds
Waylon Jennings/Jessi Colter
The O'Jays
Willie Nelson/Emmylou Harris
Mac Davis

Peaches Rock Stage

Sweetbottom
Short Stuff
Daisy Dillman Band
Paffrath & Dykhuis
The Bennett Brothers
Nantucket
Bad Boy
Mandel Machine
David Johnson
Head East
Dixie Dregs
Max Webster

Miller Jazz Oasis

Riverboat Ramblers
The Crusaders (two nights)
Roy Buchanan
Herbie Mann (two nights)
Buddy Rich (two nights)
Chick Corea (two nights)
Sonny Rollins (two nights)

Schlitz Country Scene

Grass, Food & Lodging
Doug Kershaw
Muddy Waters (two nights)
Asleep at the Wheel (two nights)
Don McLean/John Hiatt
The Amazing Rhythm Aces (two nights)
Doc Watson (two nights)
Steve Goodman/Tom Paxton

Comedy/Variety Showcase

Jay Leno (three nights)
Louis Nye (three nights)
Ace Trucking Company (three nights)
Proctor & Bergman (three nights)

Pabst International Festival

Happy Days Revue
Jay & the Americans (two nights)
Free Time Band
Tommy James (two nights)
The New Christy Minstrels
Mark Azzolina's Cavalcade of Swing
Dion (two nights)
Sound of the Coasters (two nights)

1979 *June 28-July 8*

Main Stage

Allman Brothers Band/John Hammond
Natalie Cole/Lenny Williams
Elvin Bishop and the Ozark Mountain Daredevils
Ronnie Milsap and Ray Stevens
Chic and Patti LaBelle
The Beach Boys/Iron Horse
Milwaukee Symphony Orchestra
John Davidson
Gordon Lightfoot and Crystal Gayle/Leo Kottke
Pointer Sisters/Rick Danko (Waylon Jennings canceled)
Rock N' Roll Spectacular with Jerry Lee Lewis, Danny & the Juniors, Sam & Dave, Freddy Cannon

Peaches Rock Stage

Dixie Dregs
Short Stuff
Tantrum
John Hiatt
Whiteface
Delbert McClinton
Jan Hammer
Jay Ferguson
Arroyo
Wet Willie

Miller Jazz Oasis

Stan Getz (two nights)
The Brecker Brothers (two nights)
Freddie Hubbard (two nights)
Maynard Ferguson (two nights)
Spyro Gyra
Stanley Turrentine (two nights)

Schlitz Country Scene

Piper Road Spring Band/Jerry Reed
Grass, Food & Lodging
Earl Scruggs Revue (two nights)
Pure Prairie League (two nights)
John Prine (two nights)
John Lee Hooker (two nights)
Asleep at the Wheel

Pabst International Festival

The Britins
Mary Travers (two nights)
The Drifters/The Crystals (two nights)
The Kingston Trio (two nights)
The Four Lads
Serendipity Singers
Chubby Checker (two nights)

Comedy/Variety Cabaret

Ricky Jay (three nights)
Gary Mule Deer (three nights)
Edmonds & Curley (two nights)
Henny Youngman (three nights)

Blue River Café Folk Stage

Robert "One Man" Johnson
Bill Quateman
Ron Crick
Bob Gibson
Josh White Jr.
Grass, Food & Lodging
Gil Plotkin
Corky Siegel
Bill Camplin (two nights)
James Lee Stanley

1980 *June 26-July 6*

Main Stage

Journey/Russia
Teddy Pendergrass/Crown Heights Affair
Kenny Loggins
Crystal Gayle/The Dirt Band
Jackson Browne
The Bar-Kays/GQ
Pete Seeger/Arlo Guthrie
Atlanta Rhythm Section/Levon Helm/Point Blank
Skitch Henderson/Count Basie/Milwaukee Symphony
    Orchestra
Emmylou Harris/Larry Gatlin
John Prine/Jerry Jeff Walker/Doug Kershaw (Waylon
    Jennings canceled)

Peaches Rock Stage

Squeeze
Judas Priest
Dixie Dregs
Survivor
The Hounds
Short Stuff
Sterling
Daryl Stuermer & Friends
Trillion
Yipes
Bill Bruford

Miller Jazz Oasis

Sonny Rollins (two nights)
Lionel Hampton (two nights)
Chick Corea (two nights)
Spyro Gyra (two nights)
Donald Byrd
Buddy Rich (two nights)

Schlitz Country Scene

Flying Burrito Brothers (two nights)
Earl Scruggs Revue (two nights)
New Riders of the Purple Sage (two nights)
Johnny Rodriguez & the Hole in the Wall Gang (two
    nights)
Albert King/Luther Allison
The James Cotton Band/Willie Dixon
Tracy Nelson/Heartsfield

Pabst Festival Stage

Paul Revere & the Raiders (two nights)
The Britins (two nights)
Rick Nelson (two nights)
Sam & Dave (two nights)
Chubby Checker (three nights)

Comedy/Variety Cabaret

Bob Nelson (two nights)
Kip Addotta (three nights)
Willie Tyler & Lester (three nights)
Jay Leno (three nights)

TV 24 Folk Stage

James Lee Stanley (two nights)
Robert "One Man" Johnson
Clan Gilmour
Bill Camplin
Dick Pinney
Early Sisters
Mimi Fariña (two nights)
Corky Siegel
Peter "Madcat" Ruth

1981 *June 25-July 5*

Main Stage

Allman Brothers Band/ Nighthawks
Tony Bennett
Peter, Paul & Mary
Eddie Rabbitt/Juice Newton
Pure Prairie League/Firefall/McGuffey Lane
Aretha Franklin/The Four Tops
Marshall Tucker Band/The Dregs
Cameo/Change
Glen Campbell/Terri Gibbs
Anthony Newley/Milwaukee Symphony Orchestra
George Thorogood & the Destroyers/Southside Johnny & The Asbury Jukes (Cher canceled)

WLPX/Peaches Rock Stage

The Rage
Iron Maiden
Billy Squire
Short Stuff
Sweetbottom
Bad Boy
20/20
Doc Holliday
Greg Kihn Band
Jeff Lorber's Fusion
Willie Nile

Miller Jazz Oasis

Angela Bofill (two nights)
Roy Ayers (two nights)
Spyro Gyra (two nights)
Lionel Hampton (two nights)
Pat Metheny Group (two nights)
Ramsey Lewis

Schlitz Country Scene

Ozark Mountain Daredevils (two nights)
Bill Monroe & the Bluegrass Boys
Doc and Merle Watson
Elvin Bishop (two nights)
Rosanne Cash
Muddy Waters (two nights)
Heartsfield
Asleep at the Wheel

Pabst Festival Stage

Jan & Dean (two nights)
The 5th Dimension (two nights)
The Kingston Trio (two nights)
The Britins
Chubby Checker (two nights)
Rick Nelson (two nights)

Comedy/Variety Cabaret

Joe Piscopo (two nights)
Edmonds & Curley (two nights)
Gary Mule Deer (three nights)
Bill Kirchenbauer (two nights)
Pat Paulsen (two nights)

TV6 Folk Stage

Mike Brewer
Peter "Madcat" Ruth
Early Sisters
Faith Pillow
Robert "One Man" Johnson
Gamble Rogers
Blarney
Bill Camplin
Paul Cebar
Bob Gibson
Dave Rudolf

The Steve Miller Band played on Summerfest's main stage in 1982.

1982 *June 24-July 5*

Main Stage

Bonnie Raitt/Jerry Jeff Walker/Elvin Bishop/Steve
    Goodman
The Bar-Kays/Skyy
The Steve Miller Band
The Commodores/War
Chicago/Alan Kaye
Johnny Mathis/Jeannine Burnier
Santana
The Charlie Daniels Band/Dickey Betts/Butch Trucks &
    Friends
Al Jarreau/The Larsen-Feiten Band
Arlo Guthrie/Pete Seeger
Milwaukee Symphony Orchestra
George Thorogood & the Destroyers/Gary U.S. Bonds/Joe
    Ely Band

Rock Stage

Short Stuff
Nighthawks
New Mountain with Leslie West and Corky Laing
Steel Pulse
The Rage
Bad Boy
Muscle Shoals All-Stars
The Romantics
The Rockets
Shivvers
The Mamas & the Papas
The Producers

Miller Jazz Oasis

Jeff Lorber (two nights)
Angela Bofill (two nights)
Maynard Ferguson (two nights)
Buddy Rich (two nights)
Freddie Hubbard (two nights)
Ramsey Lewis (two nights)

Schlitz Country

Pure Prairie League (two nights)
John Hartford (two nights)
Michael Murphey (two nights)
Doug Kershaw (two nights)
John Lee Hooker & the Coast to Coast Blues Band (two
    nights)
Carl Perkins (two nights)

Pabst Festival Stage

Booze Brothers Revue (two nights)
Rick Nelson (two nights)
The Britins
Paul Revere & the Raiders (two nights)
The Association (two nights)
Chubby Checker (three nights)

Comedy Cabaret

Edmonds & Curley
Ace Trucking Company (three nights)
Mack & Jamie
Marty Cohen (two nights)
Willie Tyler & Lester (two nights)
Henny Youngman (three nights)

Folk Stage

Harry Waller
Robin & Linda Williams (two nights)
Blarney
Peter Lang
Stegal & Blum
Paul Cebar
Scott Jones
Early Sisters
Peter "Madcat" Ruth
James Lee Stanley
Corky Siegel

1983 *June 30-July 10*

Main Stage

James Taylor
Kool & the Gang/The Dazz Band
Beach Boys
Rick Springfield/Sparks
Melissa Manchester/Milwaukee Symphony Orchestra
Donna Summer/Garry Shandling
Charlie Daniels Band/Marshall Tucker
Linda Ronstadt/Quarterflash
Hall & Oates/Scandal
Engelbert Humperdinck/Johnny Dark
Eric Clapton/The Blasters

Rock Stage

John Kay & Steppenwolf
Stevie Ray Vaughan & Double Trouble
Quiet Riot
R.E.M.
The Greg Kihn Band
Violent Femmes
Zebra
Josie Cotton
Donnie Iris
The Romantics
Robert Palmer

MILWAUKEE WORLD FESTIVAL INC

Paul Revere and the Raiders performed on the Pabst Festival Stage for two nights during the 1987 festival.

Miller Jazz Oasis

Jeff Lorber Fusion and Kenny G (two nights)
Larry Coryell, Mike Urbaniak, Urszula Dudziak (two nights)
Slide Hampton (two nights)
Spyro Gyra (two nights)
Maynard Ferguson (two nights)
Donald Byrd

Old Style Country

Jerry Jeff Walker (two nights)
Clarence "Gatemouth" Brown
Willie Dixon & the Chicago Blues All-Stars
Dickey Betts Band (two nights)
The Blasters (two nights)
Bill Monroe & His Blue Grass Boys
Doc & Merle Watson
John Prine & Steve Goodman

Pabst Festival Stage

Booze Brothers Revue (two nights)
Tina Turner (two nights)
Big Twist & the Mellow Fellows
Three Dog Night (two nights)
Bobby Vee, Bo Diddley (two nights)
Johnny Rivers (two nights)

Comedy Cabaret

Gary Mule Deer (two nights)
Father Guido Sarducci (two nights)
Dennis Blair (two nights)
"Weird Al" Yankovic (two nights)
Mizmo Jugglers (two nights)
Henny Youngman

Folk Stage

Chris Hillman & Al Perkins
Bob Gibson
Paul Cebar
James Lee Stanley (two nights)
Robin & Linda Williams
Peter "Madcat" Ruth
Scott Jones
Mike Brewer
Milwaukee Musicians Co-op
Heartsfield & Jordan

1984 *June 28-July 8*

Main Stage

James Taylor
Luther Vandross/The Bar-Kays
Al Jarreau
The Moody Blues
John Denver
The Pointer Sisters/Lee Ritenour
Linda Ronstadt & the Nelson Riddle Orchestra
The Go-Go's
George Thorogood & the Destroyers/The Stray Cats
The Everly Brothers
Huey Lewis & the News

Rock Stage

Daryl Stuermer & Friends
Rank and File
Talas
Colour Radio
Violent Femmes
Stevie Ray Vaughan & Double Trouble
"Weird Al" Yankovic
Streets
R.E.M.
Alcatraz
Tony Carey

Miller Jazz Oasis

Lionel Hampton (two nights)
Maynard Ferguson (two nights)
David Sanborn (two nights)
Pieces of a Dream (two nights)
Buddy Rich
Wynton Marsalis
Allan Holdsworth

Old Style Country Stage

The Marshall Tucker Band (two nights)
Vassar Clements and John Hartford (two nights)
The Greg Allman Band (two nights)
The Blasters (two nights)
John Lee Hooker & the Coast to Coast Blues Band (two nights)
Arlo Guthrie & Shenandoah

Pabst Festival Stage

Roy Orbison (two nights)
Rob Grill & the Grass Roots
B. J. Thomas
Louise Mandrell (two nights)
Big Twist & the Mellow Fellows
The Temptations (two nights)
Chubby Checker (two nights)

TV 6 Comedy Cabaret

Jay Leno (two nights)
Billy Crystal (two nights)
Willie Tyler & Lester (two nights)
Dennis Blair (two nights)
Paul Rodriguez (two nights)
The Booze Brothers

Folk Stage

Preston Reed
John Stiernberg ("Professor Bluegrass")
Milwaukee Musicians Co-op
Heartsfield & Jordan
Dave Rudolph
Gil Plotkin
The Milwaukeeans
Stegal & Blum
Peter "Madcat" Ruth

1985 *June 27-July 7*

Main Stage

Beach Boys
New Edition/Teena Marie
Survivor/Shooting Star
Eric Clapton/Graham Parker/Shot
Jimmy Buffett
Bryan Adams/Fiona
Pointer Sisters
Crystal Gayle/Milwaukee Symphony Orchestra
Kool & the Gang/Shalamar
Oak Ridge Boys/Bellamy Brothers
Kenny Loggins

Anthony Newley sang with the Milwaukee Symphony Orchestra on the main stage on July 4, 1981

Rock Stage

Helix
Robin Trower
Bon Jovi
Donnie Iris
Fabulous Thunderbirds
John Kay & Steppenwolf
Van Zant
Yngwie Malmsteen & Rising Force (two nights)
Jon Roth & Electric Sun
Violent Femmes

Miller Jazz Oasis

Maynard Ferguson (two nights)
Stanley Clarke
Steps Ahead
Spyro Gyra (two nights)
Buddy Rich (two nights)
The Yellowjackets
Wynton Marsalis
Eddie Butts

Pabst Festival Stage

Booze Brothers Revue
"Weird Al" Yankovic & His Stupid Band (two nights)
Gary Morris (two nights)
Big Twist & the Mellow Fellows
Tommy James (two nights)
Dr. Bop & the Headliners
Janie Fricke (two nights)

Old Style Country

John Prine (two nights)
Bill Monroe and the Blue Grass Boys
T.G. Sheppard
Jerry Jeff Walker (two nights)
Los Lobos
John Mayall's Bluesbreakers (two nights)
Kris Kristofferson (two nights)

Folk Stage

Preston Reed
Milwaukee Musicians Co-op
James Lee Stanley (two nights)
Johnny Aloha & Don
Paul Cebar and the Milwaukeeans
Heartsfield & Jordan
Dave Rudolf
Peter "Madcat" Ruth

TV 6 Comedy Cabaret

Tom Dreesen (two nights)
Michael Davis (two nights)
Norm Crosby (two nights)
David Steinberg
Franklyn Ajaye (two nights)
Henny Youngman (two nights)

1986 *June 26-July 6*

Main Stage

Mr. Mister/Belinda Carlisle
Violent Femmes/BoDeans/R&B Cadets
Night Ranger/Joe Walsh
Willie Nelson
Julian Lennon
Patti LaBelle
Stevie Ray Vaughan/Double Trouble/The Fabulous
    Thunderbirds
Kool & the Gang/Sly Fox
Manhattan Transfer/Milwaukee Symphony Orchestra
Billy Ocean/Meli'sa Morgan
INXS (canceled)

Rock Stage

Mink Deville
UFO
The Outlaws
John Hiatt
The Blasters
The Models
Rare Earth
The Romantics
The Suburbs
Wild Blue
Rough Cut

Miller Jazz Oasis

Herbie Hancock
Buddy Rich
Bill Kirchner
The Yellowjackets
Cabo Frio
Rodney Franklin
Maynard Ferguson (two nights)
Stanley Clarke (two nights)
Spyro Gyra

Pabst Festival Stage

The Buckinghams
Jan & Dean (two nights)
Roy Orbison (two nights)
Gerard
Three Dog Night (two nights)
Dr. Bop & the Headliners
The Coasters & the Crystals (two nights)

Old Style Country

Bonnie Raitt (two nights)
John Lee Hooker & the Coast to Coast Blues Band
Booze Brothers
Marshall Tucker Band (two nights)
The Neville Brothers
Gregg Allman & Dickey Betts (two nights)
Los Lobos (two nights)

Folk Stage

Heartsfield & Jordan
Cathy Fink
Preston Reed
Spencer Bohern
Famous Vacationers
Tony Brown
Dave Porter
David Rudolf
Roy Book Binder

TV 6 Comedy Cabaret

Sandra Bernhard (two nights)
Ed Fiala
Yakov Smirnoff (two nights)
George Kirby (two nights
The Nylons (two nights)
Louie Anderson (two nights)

1987 *June 25-July 5*

Marcus Amphitheater

Beach Boys
Bruce Hornsby & the Range
The Bangles
Dolly Parton
Paul Simon
Run-DMC
Duran Duran
Jimmy Buffett
Chicago
John Denver/Milwaukee Symphony Orchestra
Whitney Houston

Rock Stage

Andy Taylor
Stabilizers
Tesla
Jon Butcher
Ace Frehley's Comet
John Cafferty & the Beaver Brown Band
Cheap Trick
The Truth
Little America
The Bluesbusters
Richard Marx

Miller Jazz Oasis

Ramsey Lewis
Kenny G
Stanley Clarke
Med Flory & Supersax
Cabo Frio
Dirty Dozen Brass Band
Pieces of a Dream
Michael Brecker Band
Spyro Gyra (two nights)
Jeff Lorber & Karyn White

Pabst Festival Stage

Dr. Bop & the Headliners
Gene Pitney Show
The Diamonds
Paul Revere & the Raiders (two nights)
Class of '62
The Temptations
Johnny Rivers (two nights)
Sha Na Na (two nights)

Ray Davies of Kinks fame performed as a solo artist July 2, 2006, on the M&I Bank Classic Rock Stage.

JOURNAL SENTINEL

Old Style Country Stage

Emmylou Harris (two nights)
Johnny Winter (two nights)
The Booze Brothers (two nights)
Dwight Yoakam
Jason & the Scorchers
Steve Earle
The Neville Brothers (two nights)

Folk/New Age Stage

Mark Egan
The Fred Simon and David Onderdonk Group
James Lee Stanley (two nights)
Jan Marra
Scott Cossu with Van Manakas
Dave Rudolph (two nights)
Preston Reed
Tony Brown
David Arkenstone

Mix Stage

Father Guido Sarducci (two nights)
Dana Carvey (two nights)
Jim Post
Will Durst
Emo Philips
Dennis Blair (two nights)
Willie Tyler & Lester (two nights)

1988 *June 30-July 10*

Marcus Amphitheater

Stevie Wonder
Bruce Hornsby & the Range/Pat McLaughlin
Heart/Michael Bolton
John Cougar Mellencamp
Herb Alpert/Milwaukee Symphony Orchestra
Billy Ocean/Brenda Russell
George Thorogood & the Delaware Destroyers/Brian Setzer
Freddie Jackson/Natalie Cole
Steve Winwood/Savuka
Randy Travis/The Judds/David Lynn Jones
Sting

Rock Stage

Those Spanic Boys
Henry Lee Summer
The Del-Lords
Icehouse
Starship
Steppenwolf
Vinnie Vincent Invasion
The Smithereens
Steve Forbert
Gypsy
Jimmy Cliff

Miller Jazz Oasis

Maynard Ferguson & High Voltage (two shows)
Stanley Clarke
The Robert Cray Band
Third World
Oceans
The Rippingtons
The Dixie Dregs
Spyro Gyra (two nights)
Jeff Lorber

Pabst Festival Stage

Barry's Truckers
The Turtles
The Drifters and Martha Reeves (two nights)
Chubby Checker (two nights)
Jan & Dean (two nights)
Fats Domino (two nights)
Freddy Cannon and Bobby Vee

Old Style Heartland

Exile (two nights)
Lyle Lovett
k.d. lang
BoDeans (two nights)
Booze Brothers (two nights)
Siegel-Schwall Band
The Fabulous Thunderbirds (two nights)

New Age Stage

Jerry Goodman (two nights)
David Arkenstone
Uncle Festive (two nights)
Peter Kater
Samoa
Doug Cameron (two nights)
Patrick O'Hearn (two nights)

Comedy Cabaret

Dennis Miller (two nights)
Rich Hall
Will Durst (two nights)
Gilbert Gottfried (two nights)
Fred Anderson
Louie Anderson
Robert Klein (two nights)

Matilda Bay

Roomful of Blues
Danny Davis & Nashville Brass (two nights)
Buckwheat Zydeco (two nights)
Neville Brothers (two nights)
Russ Morgan Orchestra
Terrance Simien & the Mallet Playboys
Doug Kershaw (two nights)

1989 June 29-July 9

Marcus Amphitheater

Violent Femmes/New Order/Public Image Limited/
    Sugarcubes
Guy/Dino/Peabo Bryson
Hall & Oates
Jimmy Buffett/The Neville Brothers
Bob Dylan/Steve Earle
Jackson Browne/David Lindley & El Rayo-X
Paula Abdul/Lisa Lisa & Cult Jam/Tone-Loc/Milli Vanilli/
    Information Society/Was (Not Was)/Downtown Julie
    Brown/MTV Dancers
Smokey Robinson/Milwaukee Symphony Orchestra
Rod Stewart
Randy Travis/K.T. Oslin
Tom Petty & the Heartbreakers

Rock Stage

House of Lords
Robyn Hitchcock & the Egyptians
Blue Oyster Cult
Joan Jett
Warp Drive
Britny Fox
Steppenwolf
Henry Lee Summer
Sleighriders
Spirit
Red Siren

Miller Jazz Oasis

Spyro Gyra
The Yellowjackets
Paul Shaffer & the World's Most Dangerous Band (two
    nights)
Southside Johnny & the Asbury Jukes
Tower of Power
Richie Cole & Alto Madness
David Benoit
Maynard Ferguson
Blood, Sweat & Tears
Jeff Lorber

Pabst Festival Stage

Gary Puckett
The Grass Roots
Gene Pitney
The Turtles
Johnny Rivers (two nights)
Del Shannon & the Coasters
The Kingston Trio
Jan & Dean (two nights)
Paul Revere & the Raiders

Old Style Heartland Stage

The Fabulous Thunderbirds (two nights)
BoDeans (two nights)
Johnny Winter (two nights)
The Charlie Daniels Band (two nights)
Booze Brothers (two nights)
Desert Rose Band

Breezin'/Sentry Stage

Ricardo Silveira
Steve Bach
Windows
Tony Guerrero
Brian Bromberg
David Lanz (two nights)
Free Flight
David Arkenstone
Jerry Goodman (two nights)

Leinie's Chippewa Falls Tavern

The Radiators (two nights)
Wayne Toups & Zydecajun (two nights)
Dr. John (two nights)
Terrance Simien & the Mallet Playboys (two nights)
Zachary Richard
Ivan Neville (two nights)

Comedy Cabaret

Rita Rudner
Richard Belzer (two nights)
Nora Dunn
Will Durst (two nights)
Judy Tenuta (two nights)
Paul Rodriguez
Michael Winslow (two nights)

1990 *June 28-July 8*

Marcus Amphitheater

Crosby, Stills & Nash
Fleetwood Mac/Squeeze
Depeche Mode/Nitzer Ebb
Jerry Harrison/Deborah Harry/The Ramones/Tom Tom Club
Luther Vandross
Anita Baker
Richard Marx
M.C. Hammer/Troop/Michel'le/Oaktown 357
Cher/Dom Irrera
Bruce Hornsby & the Range
The B-52's/Ziggy Marley & the Melody Makers

Rock Stage

L.A. Guns
The Church
Y & T
Killer Dwarfs
Helix
Baton Rouge
Michael Penn
Hericane Alice
Peter Murphy
Lita Ford
Rick Derringer

Miller Oasis

Chick Corea Elektric Band
Tom Scott
The Robert Cray Band featuring the Memphis Horns
Maynard Ferguson & Big Bop Nouveau
Spyro Gyra
Paul Shaffer & the World's Most Dangerous Band
Richard Elliot
Roomful of Blues
Blood, Sweat & Tears featuring David Clayton-Thomas
Michael Wolff & the Posse Direct from "Arsenio Hall"
Oceans

Pabst Showcase

Barry's Truckers
Frankie Avalon (two nights)
Chubby Checker (two nights)
Meat Loaf (two nights)
Mitch Ryder & the Detroit Wheels

Old Style Heartland

Luther Allison
The Fabulous Thunderbirds (two nights)
Poco (two nights)
BoDeans (two nights)
Los Lobos (two nights)
Loey Nelson with Semi-Twang
Booze Brothers Revue

Breezin'/Sentry Stage

Rush Hour
Don Linke & Cooler Near the Lake
Aurora
Little Mel & the TKO Band
Venture
Michael Drake
World Roots
Big Shoulders
Leroy Airmaster
No Thought Required
Random Walk

Stephen Stills rocked out on guitar during the Crosby, Stills & Nash concert at the Marcus Amphitheater on June 28, 1990.

Miller Oasis

Tower of Power
The Commodores
Michael McDonald
The Rippingtons
Arrow
Richard Elliot
Jan Hammer
Spyro Gyra
Blood, Sweat & Tears featuring David Clayton-Thomas
Eddie Money
GRP All-Stars with Lee Ritenour and David Benoit

Old Style Heartland

Marshall Tucker Band (two nights)
Booze Brothers
Roger McGuinn (two nights)
Kansas (two nights)
Fabulous Thunderbirds (two nights)
The Band (two nights)

Pabst Showcase

Barry's Truckers
The Temptations (two nights)
Frankie Valli & the Four Seasons (two nights)
The Guess Who
Davy Jones of the Monkees
The Turtles (two nights)
The New Rascals
Jan & Dean

Rock Stage

Blue Oyster Cult
Tyketto
Shooting Star
Saraya
The Replacements
John Kay & Steppenwolf
House of Lords
Rhino Bucket
Dangerous Toys
DiVinyls
Drivin' n' Cryin'

Leinie's Lodge

C.J. Chenier
Terrance Simien & the Mallet Playboys (two nights)
Dirty Dozen Brass Band (two nights)
Dr. John (two nights)
Buckwheat Zydeco (two nights)
Wayne Toups & Zydecajun (two nights)

Comedy Cabaret

Carl Strong
Kevin Pollack
Robert Wuhl
Rip Tenor/Gilbert Gottfried
Paula Poundstone
Will Durst/Lewis Black (two nights)
Robert Klein (two nights)
Emo Philips (two nights)

1991 *June 27-July 7*

Marcus Amphitheater

Whitney Houston/After 7
Tesla/Slaughter
Violent Femmes/Fishbone/Jellyfish
Warrant/Trixter/Firehouse
Hank Williams Jr. & the Bama Band/The Kentucky Headhunters
Michael Bolton/ Keedy
Bell Biv DeVoe/Tony! Toni! Tone!/C + C Music Factory/ Gerardo/Tara Kemp
The Judds/McBride & the Ride
Huey Lewis & the News/The Subdudes
Julio Iglesias
Jimmy Buffett/Fingers Taylor & the Lady Fingers Band

Leinie's Lodge

The Dirty Dozen Brass Band (two nights)
Wayne Toups & Zydecajun
Dr. John & Band (two nights)
Leon Russell
Spanic Boys
Buckwheat Zydeco (two nights)
Bruce Daigrepont
Terrance Simien & the Mallet Playboys

Pabst 'Blue Ribbon Blues' Stage

Albert King
Bobby "Blue" Bland
Koko Taylor
Otis Rush
Clarence "Gatemouth" Brown
Kinsey Report
Lonnie Brooks
Magic Slim
Elvin Bishop (two nights)
Junior Wells

Comedy Cabaret

Paul Rodriguez (two nights)
Night at the Improv with Budd Friedman, Bobby Collins,
   John Wing, Ron Pearson (two nights)
Emo Philips
Will Durst (two nights)
Carl Strong (two nights)
Paula Poundstone (two nights)

1992 *June 25-July 5*

Marcus Amphitheater

Ringo Starr & His All-Starr Band
Clint Black/Aaron Tippin
The Steve Miller Band
Crosby, Stills & Nash
John Mellencamp
Metallica
Jimmy Buffett
Warren Zevon, Roger McGuinn, BoDeans
Michael Bolton
Jodeci
Paula Abdul/Color Me Badd

Miller Oasis

Kenny Loggins (two nights)
Peter Frampton
Ronnie Laws/Philip Bailey/Rodney Franklin
Richard Elliot
King Sunny Ade
Neville Brothers
Robert Cray
Reggae Sunsplash
Southside Johnny & the Asbury Jukes

Old Style Heartland

Indigo Girls/Matthew Sweet
Arc Angels/Sass Jordan
Allman Brothers
Jukebox Heroes
Marshall Tucker Band (two nights)
Kentucky Headhunters
Poco
Tower of Power
48th Street Rockers
Bela Fleck & the Flecktones

Pabst Showcase

Barry's Truckers
Tommy James
Peter Frampton
The Four Tops (two nights)
Jefferson Starship
Chubby Checker
Jan & Dean
The Temptations (two nights)
B.T.O.

WLZR/Mainstream Rock Stage

Lillian Axe
The Storm
King's X
Lynch Mob
Webb Wilder Band
Bangalore Choir
Charlatans U.K.
John Kay & Steppenwolf

Pabst 'Blue Ribbon Blues'

The Nighthawks
Junior Wells
The Professor with A.C. Reed and Mighty Joe Young
Little Charlie & the Nightcats with John Hammond Jr.
Rod Piazza & the Mighty Flyers
Koko Taylor & Her Blues Machine
Elvin Bishop
The Charlie Musselwhite Band
Danny Gatton
Gatemouth Brown
Otis Clay and Ann Peebles with the Memphis Hi Section

Leinie Lodge

Michael Doucet & Beausoleil
Paul Cebar & the Milwaukeeans
Alejandro Escovedo
Terrance Simien
The Radiators
Irma Thomas & the Professionals
Buckwheat Zydeco (two nights)
The Roches
Wayne Toups & Zydecajun
The Iguanas

Comedy Cabaret

Judy Tenuta
Richard Belzer
Brady Street Comedy Troupe
John Mendoza
Michael Winslow
Will Durst (two nights)
Gary Mule Deer
Bobcat Goldthwait
Pauly Shore (two nights)

1993 *June 24-July 4*

Marcus Amphitheater

Sting/dada
Tina Turner/Lindsey Buckingham
Arrested Development/Gumbo
Don Henley
Patti LaBelle/LeVert/Silk
Jimmy Buffett/The Iguanas
The Moody Blues/Milwaukee Symphony Orchestra
Spin Doctors/Soul Asylum/Screaming Trees
Bruce Hornsby/BoDeans
Dwight Yoakam/Suzy Bogguss
Bon Jovi/Extreme

Miller Oasis

Java
Glenn Frey/Joe Walsh Band
Los Lobos
Shadowfax
Grover Washington Jr.
Hugh Masekela
Jellyfish/Material Issue/Antenna
Reggae Sunsplash - World Peace Tour
Jon Secada
War
Richard Elliot

Old Style Heartland

The Kentucky Headhunters
Johnny Johnson & the Kentucky Headhunters
America
Pirates of the Mississippi
Big Head Todd & the Monsters
The Jayhawks
Nitty Gritty Dirt Band
Buddy Guy (two nights)
John Anderson
Kansas

Pabst Showcase

Barry's Truckers
Paul Revere & the Raiders
Dion
Bo Diddley
The Temptations (two nights)
Steppenwolf
Sammy Kershaw
The Everly Brothers (two nights)
"Weird Al" Yankovic

LAZER 103/Mainstream Rock Stage

Robin Trower
Enuff Z'Nuff
Jackyl
Great White
Trixter
Dream Theater
Triumph
Wild Side
Arcade
Smithereens
Bullet Boys

Pabst 'Blue Ribbon Blues'

Albert Collins & the Icebreakers
Billy Flynn's Blues All-Stars
Red Devils
Lonnie Brooks Blues Band
Ramsey Lewis
Jim Liban
Koko Taylor & Her Blues Machine
John Mayall & the Blues Breakers (two nights)
Bobby "Blue" Bland
Dr. John

Marcia Ball (right) played the blues at the Potawatomi Bingo Casino Stage on June 30, 2002. Pat Boyack played guitar.

Fred Schneider of the B-52's got zany while performing at the Marcus Amphitheater on July 8, 1990.

Leinie Lodge

John Hiatt and Band
Wayne Toups & Zydecajun
Bluerunners
Johnny Clegg & Savuka
Texas Tornados (two nights)
Paul Cebar & the Milwaukeeans
Evangeline
Nathan & the Zydeco Cha-Chas
Rockin' Dopsie & the Zydeco Twisters
Zachary Richard

Comedy Cabaret

Richard Belzer (two nights)
Emo Philips
Brady Street Comedy Troupe
Carrot Top
Will Durst with Deb & Mike (two nights)
Gilbert Gottfried
Carl Strong
Carol Leifer/Wendy Liebman/Caroline Rhea
Bobcat Goldthwait

1994 *June 30-July 10*

Marcus Amphitheater

Yes
Metallica/Danzig/Suicidal Tendencies
Soundgarden/Eleven/TAD/Jeff Buckley
Salt 'N Pepa/R. Kelly/K7/The Puppies
BoDeans/Roger McGuinn
Janet Jackson/MC Lyte
Traffic/Sonia Dada
Depeche Mode/Primal Scream/Stabbing Westward
Bonnie Raitt/Bruce Hornsby
Brooks & Dunn/Faith Hill
Stone Temple Pilots/Meat Puppets/Redd Kross

Miller Oasis

Los Lobos (two nights)
Little Feat
Santana
Tower of Power
Mahlathini & the Mahotella Queens
Dave Koz
Brian Setzer Orchestra
Kenny Loggins (two nights)
Marcia Ball

Old Style Heartland

Dixie Dregs
Kansas (two nights)
Buddy Guy (two nights)
Tina & the B-Side Movement
Loverboy
ELO (Part II)
Dan Seals
Jimmie Vaughan
Jimi Jamison's Survivor

Pabst Showcase

Barry's Truckers
Patty Loveless
The Temptations (two nights)
Steppenwolf
Peter Frampton (two nights)
Sammy Kershaw
The Grass Roots
Aaron Tippin
Confederate Railroad

LAZER 103/Mainstream Rock Stage

Brother Cane
Blackfoot
Candlebox
Great White
Cry of Love
Anthrax
Cheap Trick
Robin Trower
Dio

93 QFM Leinie Lodge

Beausoleil avec Michael Doucet
Collective Soul
Buckwheat Zydeco
Spanic Boys
Paul Cebar & the Milwaukeeans
The Lemonheads
Smithereens
King Sunny Ade
Dirty Dozen Brass Band
The Band

Potawatomi Casino Soul Stage

Mint Condition
Harvey Scales & the Seven Sounds
Glenn Jones
Kenny Kotwitz Quartet featuring Mary Kotwitz
The Bar-Kays
Shirley Murdock
Charlie Musselwhite
Black Earth Plus
Lonnie Brooks Blues Band
Impacto Tropical
Blind Boys of Alabama featuring Clarence Fountain

Comedy Brew Pub

Rob Schneider (two nights)
Will Durst (two nights)
Bobby Collins
Drew Carey
Lewis Black
Kevin Nealon/Julia Sweeney with ComedySportz (two nights)
Jon Stewart
Carl Strong

1995 *June 29-July 9*

Marcus Amphitheater

Bonnie Raitt/Charles Brown/Ruth Brown
BoDeans/Lowen & Navarro
Vince Gill
Seal/Des'ree
Luther Vandross
Randy Travis/Jeff Foxworthy
Hootie & the Blowfish/The Freddy Jones Band
Boyz II Men/Adina Howard
Michael Bolton
Pearl Jam/Bad Religion (two nights)

Miller Oasis

Marcia Ball
Reggae Sunsplash '95: Aswad, Dennis Brown, Buju Banton, Wailing Souls, Sister Carol, Worl-A-Girl, Junior Tucker, Skool Band, Christafari, Tommy Cowan
Little Feat
Tom Jones
Ringo Starr & His All-Starr Band
The Iguanas
Dave Alvin & the Skeletons
Jeff Healey Band
Fleetwood Mac
Spyro Gyra
Roomful of Blues

Old Style Heartland

Vic Ferrari Band
Starship (featuring Mickey Thomas)
"Texas Roadhouse Jam" featuring Doyle Bramhall, Omar & the Howlers, The Fabulous Thunderbirds
REO Speedwagon (two nights)
Jukebox Heroes (reunion)
The Jayhawks
Kansas (two nights)
John Anderson
Booze Brothers Show Band

Pabst Showcase

Barry's Truckers (two nights)
Chubby Checker
John Kay & Steppenwolf
The Mavericks
Pam Tillis
Confederate Railroad (two nights)
The Guess Who
The Tractors
Trisha Yearwood

LAZER 103 Rock Stage

Corrosion of Conformity
Ian Moore
Cinderella
Dokken
Extreme
Urge Overkill
Cheap Trick
Goo Goo Dolls
Brother Cane

93 QFM Leinie Lodge

Zachary Richard
Sonny Landreth
General Public
The Gufs
Stone Roses
The Radiators
Sponge
Tragically Hip
Blue Rodeo
Paul Cebar & the Milwaukeeans

Potawatomi Casino Blues/Soul Stage

The Bar-Kays (two nights)
Sam Moore
John Mayall
Larry McCray
Blind Boys of Alabama featuring Clarence Fountain
Aaliyah
O.J. Ekemode & the Nigerian All-Stars
Clarence "Gatemouth" Brown
The Staple Singers
Lucky Dube

Comedy Stage

Bobby Collins
George Wallace
Rondell Sheridan
Rhonda Shear
Lewis Black
Carl Strong
Bobcat Goldthwait
Will Durst (two nights)
Margaret Smith
Gilbert Gottfried

1996 *June 27-July 7*

Marcus Amphitheater

Alanis Morissette/Loud Lucy
BoDeans/John Hiatt
Coolio/SWV/Monica
Def Leppard/Tripping Daisy
Dwight Yoakam/David Ball
Meat Loaf
Alabama/Dan Seals
Violent Femmes/Goo Goo Dolls/Dishwalla
Aretha Franklin/Milwaukee Symphony Orchestra
R. Kelly/L.L. Cool J/Xscape/Men of Vizion
H.O.R.D.E. Festival with Blues Traveler, Lenny Kravitz, Rusted Root, Natalie Merchant

Miller Oasis

War
Tower of Power
Little Feat
The Rembrandts
The Average White Band
Eddie Money
Delbert McClinton
Robert Cray Band
Brian Setzer Orchestra
Roomful of Blues

Old Style Heartland

The Love Monkeys
Creedence Clearwater Revisited (two nights)
Jerry Jeff Walker
Vic Ferrari Band
Ted Nugent (two nights)
Booze Brothers
Poi Dog Pondering
Tina & the B-Side Movement
Molly Hatchet

Pabst Showcase

Barry's Truckers (two nights)
David Clayton-Thomas with Blood, Sweat & Tears
John Kay & Steppenwolf
Truckers Revue
David Lee Murphy
Bryan White
Three Dog Night
Confederate Railroad
Survivor featuring Jimi Jamison
Doug Supernaw

LAZER 103 Rock Stage

Stabbing Westward
The Hunger
Seven Mary Three
Ian Moore Band
Screamin' Cheetah Wheelies
Gravity Kills
The Verve Pipe
Brother Cane
The Gufs
Everclear
The Nixons

Leinie Lodge

The Tragically Hip
Freddy Jones Band
Pete Droge
The Radiators
Wilco
Imperial Drag
The Subdudes
Buckwheat Zydeco
Del Amitri
Citizen King

Potawatomi Casino Blues & Soul Stage

Blind Boys of Alabama featuring Clarence Fountain
Robben Ford & the Blue Line
Wailing Souls
Larry McCray
Taj Mahal
Duke Robillard Band with John Hammond
Zapp & Roger
The Staple Singers
Siegel-Schwall Band
Tabu Ley Rochereau el L'Orchestre Afrisa International
Fast Company

Comedy Stage

George Wallace
Wendy Liebman
Norm MacDonald
Brian Regan
Lewis Black
Will Durst (two nights)
Kevin Meaney
Carl Strong
Mark Curry
Gabe Kaplan

1997 June 26-July 6

Marcus Amphitheater

Dave Matthews Band/Los Lobos
Bush/The Jesus Lizard/Souls
John Mellencamp/Amanda Marshall
Tina Turner/Cyndi Lauper
The Moody Blues/Milwaukee Symphony Orchestra
New Edition
No Doubt/Weezer/Face to Face
Counting Crows/The Wallflowers
Tim McGraw/Martina McBride
Blackstreet/Changing Faces/Jay-Z
James Taylor

Miller Oasis

Zachary Richard
Black Uhurú
Little Feat
Los Lobos
Marcia Ball
Steve Azar
Daryl Stuermer
Huey Lewis & the News
Widespread Panic (two nights)
Neville Brothers

Briggs & Stratton Heartland Stage

The Love Monkeys (two nights)
The Tubes with Fee Waybill
.38 Special (two nights)
REO Speedwagon (two nights)
Southern Culture on the Skids
Big Head Todd & the Monsters
The Jayhawks
Poi Dog Pondering

Harley-Davidson Roadhouse

Chaka Khan
Joe Walsh
Lyle Lovett & His Large Band
The Marshall Tucker Band
Guitars, Sax & More featuring Rick Braun, Craig Chaquico, Richard Elliot and Peter White
Jim Belushi & the Sacred Hearts Band
Joe Diffie
Cheap Trick
Mint Condition
Foo Fighters
Vic Ferrari Band

Rock Stage

Helmet
Orbit
Stir
The Nixons
Seven Mary Three
Gravity Kills
The Hunger
The Gufs
Collective Soul

JOURNAL SENTINEL

DJ Gretchen spins at the Harley-Davidson Roadhouse on July 6, 2006.

Leinie Lodge

Soul Asylum
Buckwheat Zydeco
Local H
Citizen King
The Nixons
The Caulfields
The Why Store
The Freddy Jones Band
La Mafia
John Hiatt
Matthew Sweet

Sprecher Rhythm & Brews Stage

McTavish
The Bar-Kays
Willy Porter
Bobby "Blue" Bland
Zapp & Roger
Chubby Carrier & the Bayou Swamp Band
Luther Allison
Robin Trower
John Mayall & the Bluesbreakers
Lonnie Mack
Paul Cebar & the Milwaukeeans

Pepsi Comedy Stage

Bobby Collins
Victoria Jackson
Lewis Black
Chris Barnes & Carl Strong
Rondell Sheridan
Mitch Mullany
Will Durst (two nights)
Jeff Dunham
Jim Breuer
Tommy Davidson

1998 *June 25-July 5*

Marcus Amphitheater

BoDeans/Big Head Todd & the Monsters
Phil Collins Big Band
Boyz II Men/Next/Destiny's Child/Mya/Uncle Sam
Kenny G
Bonnie Raitt/Little Feat
LeAnn Rimes/Bryan White
Mary J. Blige/Brian McKnight/Xscape
Widespread Panic/G. Love & Special Sauce/Leftover Salmon/Todd Snider & the Nervous Wrecks
Shania Twain
James Taylor
Smashing Pumpkins/Hum

Miller Oasis

The Love Monkeys
Violent Femmes
Ziggy Marley & the Melody Makers
The Radiators
Heart featuring Ann Wilson
Keb' Mo'
Brian Setzer Orchestra
Chumbawamba
K.C. & the Sunshine Band
Tonic
Marcia Ball

Briggs & Stratton Big Backyard

Showdown
Lee Ritenour
Smokey Robinson
The Booze Brothers
Chicago
Gene Pitney
REO Speedwagon (two nights)
Third Eye Blind
Ramsey Lewis
The Jayhawks

Harley-Davidson Roadhouse

Smash Mouth
The Gufs
Cherry Poppin' Daddies
The Temptations
Daryl Hall & John Oates
John Kay and Steppenwolf
BlackHawk
Teen Idols: Davy Jones, Bobby Sherman & Peter Noone
Jonny Lang
Foreigner
Cameo

Rock Stage

Brother Cane
Candlebox
Monster Magnet
Jimmie's Chicken Shack
Addict
Stabbing Westward
Gravity Kills
Seven Mary Three
Creed
Chris Duarte
Spacehog

Leinie Lodge

Sister Hazel
Buckwheat Zydeco
Albita
Semisonic
Pat Benatar
Sprung Monkey
K's Choice
The Freddy Jones Band
The Iguanas
Wilco
The Mighty Blue Kings

Sprecher/House Of Blues Stage

Inner Circle
The Dirty Dozen
Willy Porter
Lonnie Brooks
Morris Day & the Time
Terrance Simien
The Fabulous Thunderbirds
Big Bad Voodoo Daddy
Koko Taylor & Her Blues Machine
Paul Cebar & the Milwaukeeans
Roots Rock Society

Pepsi Comedy Pavilion

John Caponera
John Henton
Maryellen Hooper
Bobby Collins
Lewis Black
Will Durst (two nights)
Chris Barnes
Tommy Davidson
Darrell Hammond
John Pinette

1999 *June 24-July 4*

Marcus Amphitheater

Rod Stewart
BoDeans/Chris Isaak
Violent Femmes/Citizen King/The Promise Ring
R. Kelly/Foxy Brown
Dave Matthews Band/The Iguanas
Alan Jackson/Andy Griggs
Lauryn Hill
Brandy/Tyrese/Silk/C-Note
John Mellencamp/Son Volt
Lynyrd Skynyrd/Kenny Wayne Shepherd
Paul Simon and Bob Dylan

Miller Oasis

The Boogie Men
Jimmy Cliff
The Freddy Jones Band
Sonia Dada
The Why Store
Delbert McClinton
.38 Special
Neville Brothers
The B-52's
Brian Setzer Orchestra
The Love Monkeys

Briggs & Stratton Big Backyard

Love Monkeys
Big Head Todd & the Monsters
The Village People
Eric Burdon & the New Animals
George Benson
REO Speedwagon
Foreigner
Hootie & the Blowfish (two nights)
Boz Scaggs
Ziggy Marley & the Melody Makers

Leinie Lodge

Joey McIntyre
Willy Porter
The Freddy Jones Band
Robert Cray Band featuring the Memphis Horns
Vonda Shepard
Semisonic
Everything
Reel Big Fish
Shawn Mullins
Jimmie Vaughan
Peter Himmelman

Harley-Davidson Roadhouse

Morris Day & the Time
Tony! Toni! Toné!
Chicago
Los Lobos
Pat Benatar
Deana Carter
Journey
Little Feat
The Booze Brothers Show Band
Buddy Guy
Doobie Brothers

Rock Stage

Local H
Powerman 5000
Econoline Crush
Soulmaster
Second Coming
Silverchair
The Verve Pipe
The Gufs (two nights)
Joe Strummer
Collective Soul

Potawatomi Casino Stage

War
Buckwheat Zydeco
Southside Johnny & the Asbury Jukes
Dark Star Orchestra
John Mayall & the Bluesbreakers
Royal Crown Revue
The Rippingtons
The Average White Band
Steve Riley & the Mamou Playboys
Paul Cebar & the Milwaukeeans
Susan Tedeschi

Pepsi Comedy Pavilion

Carl Strong
Dave Chappelle
Jeff Cesario
John Witherspoon
Lewis Black
Wendy Liebman
Joe Rogan
Judy Tenuta
Will Durst/Deb & Mike
The Amazing Jonathan
George Lopez

2000 *June 29-July 9*

Marcus Amphitheater

Jimmy Page & the Black Crowes
Allman Brothers Band/Susan Tedeschi
Christina Aguilera
Red Hot Chili Peppers/Foo Fighters/Blonde Redhead
Blink-182/Bad Religion/Fenix TX
D'Angelo/Eric Benet
Don Henley
Brian McKnight/Milwaukee Symphony Orchestra
No Doubt/Lit/Black Eyed Peas
Britney Spears
BoDeans/Big Head Todd & the Monsters

Miller Oasis

The Love Monkeys
Todd Rundgren
Ringo Starr & His All-Starr Band
The Edgar Winter Band
Brian Setzer Orchestra
Matthew Sweet
Marcia Ball
Wailing Souls
Violent Femmes
Michael McDonald
Ben Folds Five

Briggs & Stratton Big Backyard

Indigo Girls
Morris Day & the Time/Maceo Parker
Al Green
"Weird Al" Yankovic
Spyro Gyra
Isaac Hayes
REO Speedwagon
Barry's Truckers
Peter Frampton
Third Eye Blind
The Love Monkeys

Harley-Davidson Roadhouse

Blues Traveler
Citizen King
Tito Puente Band with Pete Escovedo & Eddie Palmieri
Buddy Guy/Taj Mahal & the Phantom Blues
George Thorogood & the Destroyers
The Boogie Men
Styx
Cheap Trick
Dwight Yoakam
Montell Jordan
Kansas

Rock Stage

Deftones
Pushmonkey
Sebastian Bach
Filter
Sevendust
3 Doors Down
The Nixons
Stroke 9
Veruca Salt
The Gufs
Jesse James Dupree

Leinie Lodge

C.J. Chenier & the Red Hot Louisiana Band
Cowboy Mouth
Ben Harper & the Innocent Criminals
Goldfinger
John Hiatt & the Goners
Sister Hazel
Paula Cole
Medeski Martin & Wood
Willy Porter/Shannon Curfman
Vertical Horizon
La Bottine Souriante

Potawatomi Casino Stage

Steel Pulse
Roger McGuinn
Ozomatli
Indigenous
Robin Trower
KC & the Sunshine Band
Lonnie Brooks
Bo Diddley
Dark Star Orchestra
The Radiators
The Funky Meters

Pepsi Comedy Pavilion

Kathleen Madigan
Harland Williams
Bobby Collins
Apollo Night at Summerfest
Hugh Donaldson/Chris Barnes
Carlos Mencia
Jimmie Walker
Jim Breuer
Will Durst/Deb & Mike
Lewis Black
Joey Kola

Michelle Shocked played at the Potawatomi Casino Stage on June 30, 2003.

JOURNAL SENTINEL

2001 *June 28-July 8*

Marcus Amphitheater

Prince
Paul Simon/Brian Wilson
BoDeans/Joan Osborne
Poison/Warrant/Quiet Riot/Enuff Z'Nuff
Destiny's Child/True Vibe/Stacie Orrico
Widespread Panic/Ben Harper & the Innocent Criminals
Tom Petty & the Heartbreakers
Blink-182/New Found Glory
3 Doors Down/Lifehouse/Tantric
Tim McGraw/Kenny Chesney
Bon Jovi

Miller Oasis

Little Feat
Violent Femmes
Tower of Power
Oleander
Tonic
A Walk Down Abbey Road Starring Alan Parsons, Ann Wilson, Todd Rundgren, John Entwistle
Dogstar
The Love Monkeys
David Crosby & CPR
Everclear
Blues Traveler

Briggs & Stratton Big Backyard

Beach Boys
Toga Nite with Otis Day & the Knights
James Brown
Dave Koz & Friends
Three Dog Night
The Cult
Cameo
Sonia Dada
Jamie O'Neal
The Love Monkeys
The Wallflowers

Harley-Davidson Roadhouse

G. Love & Special Sauce
Susan Tedeschi
Jessica Andrews
Jonny Lang
Slash's Snakepit
Morris Day & the Time
Mary Chapin Carpenter
Ambrosia with Gary Wright, Dave Mason & Colin Hay
An Evening of Guitar and Saxes featuring Craig Chaquico
Doobie Brothers
Vertical Horizon

Mountain Dew Rock Stage

Cheap Trick
The Gufs
Days of the New
Spacehog
Seven Mary Three
Monster Magnet
Stabbing Westward
Tesla
Saliva
The Toadies
Union Underground

Leinie Lodge

moe.
Dr. John
Willy Porter
Uncle Kracker
Wilco
Reel Big Fish
Dark Star Orchestra
Semisonic
Black Eyed Peas
The Jayhawks
R&B Cadets

Potawatomi Casino Stage

Short Stuff
Maxi Priest
Buckwheat Zydeco
The Radiators
Indigenous
Legends of Rock n' Roll impersonator show
Cubanismo/Barbarito Torres
Charlie Musselwhite
Femi Kuti
The Big Wu
Bobby Rush

Pepsi Comedy Pavilion

Jake Johannsen
Richard Jeni
Tracy Morgan
Apollo Night at Summerfest
Will Durst/Deb & Mike
Jeff Cesario
John Witherspoon
Lewis Black
Rene Hicks
Chris Barnes and Preacher Moss
Aries Spears

2002 *June 27-July 7*

Marcus Amphitheater

Sheryl Crow/Jars of Clay
Phil Lesh & Friends/Allman Brothers Band/Lucinda Williams
Brooks & Dunn/Dwight Yoakam/Gary Allan/Chris Cagel/Trick Pony
Tom Petty & the Heartbreakers/Brian Setzer Trio
BoDeans/Train
Alicia Keys/Musiq
Widespread Panic/Galactic/J.J. Cale
Nickelback/Jerry Cantrell
John Mellencamp/Shannon McNally
Kenny Chesney/Montgomery Gentry/Jamie O'Neal/Phil Vassar
Eagles

Miller Lite Oasis

The Love Monkeys
Better Than Ezra
The B-52's
Five for Fighting
The Brothers Johnson
Soul Asylum
Live
Our Lady Peace
Blondie
Sugar Ray
Violent Femmes

Briggs & Stratton Big Backyard

Heart — Ann & Nancy Wilson
Ray Charles
The Four Tops
The Love Monkeys
INXS
Earth, Wind & Fire
A Walk Down Abbey Road starring Todd Rundgren, Alan Parsons, Christopher Cross, Mark Farner, Jack Bruce
Boney James
Ted Nugent
Carolyn Dawn Johnson
Big Head Todd & the Monsters

Harley-Davidson Roadhouse

Filter
Keith Urban
Tonic
Nappy Roots
Indigo Girls
Jewel
Maxi Priest
Tweet
Los Lobos
G. Love & Special Sauce
George Thorogood & the Destroyers

Mountain Dew Rock Stage

Sevendust
Tantric
The Buzzhorn
Local H
The Gufs
Andrew W.K.
Default
Tommy Lee
Lit
Custom
Judas Priest

Piggly Wiggly Musicmarket

Ben Folds
Willy Porter
Bela Fleck & the Flecktones/Nickel Creek
The Promise Ring/Guided by Voices
War
Big Bad Voodoo Daddy
Nitty Gritty Dirt Band
O.A.R.
Lifehouse
Dark Star Orchestra recreates the Jerry Garcia Band

Potawatomi Casino Stage

The Big Wu
Buddy Guy
Buckwheat Zydeco
Third World
The Radiators
Legends of Rock & Roll impersonator show
Junior Brown
Rusted Root
Midnight Oil
Femi Kuti

99 WMYX Comedy Pavilion

Frank Caliendo
Maryellen Hooper
Bobby Collins
Will Durst/Deb & Mike
Lewis Black
Chris Barnes/Eric O'Shea
Gilbert Gottfried
Carl Strong
Carl Banks
ComedySportz
Apollo Night at Summerfest

2003 *June 26-July 6*

Marcus Amphitheater

Peter Gabriel/Sevara Nazarkhan
Ben Harper and the Innocent Criminals/Jack Johnson
Tom Petty & the Heartbreakers/Bo Diddley
Fleetwood Mac
Foo Fighters/Pete Yorn
The Dead/Willie Nelson & Family
Toby Keith/Blake Shelton
BoDeans/Guster
Santana/Angelique Kidjo
Kenny Chesney/Keith Urban/Deana Carter
Good Charlotte/Hoobastank

Miller Lite Oasis

Eddie Butts Band
Default
Everclear
Eve 6
The Love Monkeys
Dirty Dozen Brass Band
Reverend Horton Heat
Jonny Lang
Collective Soul
David Lee Roth
Dennis DeYoung

Briggs & Stratton Big Backyard

Neville Brothers
LL Cool J
Little Richard
Blues Traveler
The Moody Blues
The Fabulous Thunderbirds
Phil Vassar
Michelle Branch
The Funk Brothers
Rick Braun
The Love Monkeys

Frank Caliendo, a Waukesha native, got laughs in the 99 WMYX Comedy Pavilion on June 27, 2002.

Harley-Davidson Roadhouse

Creedence Clearwater Revisited
Buddy Guy
Sum 41
Dark Star Orchestra
Joe Cocker
India.Arie
Savoy Brown featuring Kim Simmonds
George Thorogood & the Destroyers
Black Eyed Peas
Morris Day & the Time
Evanescence

Mountain Dew Rock Stage

Local H
RA
Sevendust
Powerman 5000
Andrew W.K.
Taproot
Mudvayne
Trapt
Quiet Riot
(Hed) Pe
Saliva

Piggly Wiggly Musicmarket

Steel Pulse
Willy Porter Band
Arturo Sandoval
Spyro Gyra
The Saw Doctors
Rusted Root
Ben Folds
O.A.R.
John Hiatt
Common
The Jayhawks

Potawatomi Casino Stage

Blind Boys of Alabama
The Funky Meters
Tito Nieves and Orquestra
Lucky Dube
The Radiators
Buckwheat Zydeco
Jerry Jeff Walker
John Mayall & the Bluesbreakers
Dickey Betts & Great Southern
Shemekia Copeland
Los Lobos

North Shore Bank Landing

"Weird" Al Yankovic
Steve Winwood
Nitty Gritty Dirt Band
Cheap Trick
The Big Wu
Paul Cebar & the Milwaukeeans
Reel Big Fish
Wilco
DJ Ken Jordan & DJ Scott Kirkland of the Crystal Method
The Boogie Men
The Wallflowers

2004 *June 24-July 4*

Marcus Amphitheater

Prince & the New Power Generation
Kid Rock/Twisted Brown Trucker/Puddle of Mudd
Kenny Chesney/Uncle Kracker
Big Boi/Ludacris/Twista
Blink-182/Motion City Soundtrack
Jessica Simpson/Ryan Cabrera
Nickelback/3 Doors Down/Thornley
Steve Miller/BoDeans
John Mayer/Maroon 5/DJ Logic
Crosby, Stills & Nash
Tim McGraw/Big & Rich/The Warren Brothers

Miller Oasis

The Darkness
LeAnn Rimes
Live
Fountains of Wayne
Something Corporate
Better Than Ezra
Pat Benatar & Neil Giraldo
Pyromania (Def Leppard tribute)
Talib Kweli
311
Fuel

Briggs & Stratton Big Backyard

Clarence Clemmons Temple of Soul
Dion
David Clayton-Thomas with Blood, Sweat & Tears
The Isley Brothers featuring Ronald Isley
Joan Jett & the Blackhearts
The Love Monkeys
Kool & the Gang
Peter Frampton
The Used
Kim Waters
Indigo Girls

Harley-Davidson Roadhouse

Liz Phair
Guster
Frankie Negron
Jason Mraz
Morris Day & the Time
Kenny Wayne Shepherd
Loverboy
The Ataris
Craig Chaquico
The Roots
Jet

Mountain Dew Rock Stage

Seether
Chevelle
Tantric
Hairball, "A spoof on '80s rock"
Drowning Pool
Saliva
Tesla
Damageplan
Trapt
Shinedown
Three Days Grace

Piggly Wiggly Musicmarket

The Big Wu
Ben Folds/Rufus Wainwright
Sister Hazel
The Flatlanders (featuring Butch Hancock, Jimmie Dale
    Gilmore and Joe Ely)
The Tubes featuring Fee Waybill
Galactic
The Fixx
Willy Porter
Switchfoot
Medeski Martin & Wood
The Johnny Clegg Band featuring the music of Juluka and
    Savuka

Potawatomi Casino Stage

Phil Vassar
moe.
Asleep at the Wheel
Tower of Power
Femi Kuti
Cheap Trick
Gin Blossoms
Los Lobos
Shelby Lynne
Taj Mahal & the Hula Blues
The Radiators

North Shore Bank Landing

Night Ranger
Buddy Guy
An Evening with O.A.R.
Buckwheat Zydeco
Dark Star Orchestra
Burning Spear
Styx
Paul Oakenfold
Dashboard Confessional
Rick Springfield
Five for Fighting

**The Dirty Dozen
Brass Band:
Harley-Davidson
Roadhouse
July 2, 2005**

2005 *June 30-July 10*

Marcus Amphitheater

John Mellencamp/John Fogerty
Tom Petty & the Heartbreakers/The Black Crowes
Kenny Chesney/Gretchen Wilson/Pat Green
Santana/Los Lonely Boys/Salvador Santana Band
Stevie Nicks/Vanessa Carlton
The Allman Brothers/Derek Trucks Band/Gov't Mule
Journey
Pixies/Weezer/The Fray
BoDeans/Wallflowers/Anna Nalick
Tim McGraw/Keith Urban/Hot Apple Pie
James Taylor

Miller Lite Oasis

Deep Purple
Rusted Root
Pat Green
Moby
Ben Folds
Kool & the Gang
Violent Femmes
Kenny Wayne Shepherd
The Donnas
Collective Soul
Better Than Ezra

Briggs & Stratton Big Backyard

LeAnn Rimes
Johnny Rivers
Dave Mason
Lucinda Williams
Robert Randolph & the Family Band
Steel Pulse
String Cheese Incident
The Ohio Players
Phil Vassar
.38 Special
Fantasia

Harley-Davidson Roadhouse

Morris Day & the Time
Sugar Ray
Dr. John/Dirty Dozen Brass Band
Howie Day
Little Feat
John Hiatt & the North Mississippi Allstars
Craig Morgan
Death Cab for Cutie
Isaac Hayes
O.A.R.
Dark Star Orchestra

Mountain Dew Rock Stage

Chevelle
Crossfade
Theory of a Deadman/Submersed
Shinedown
Bret Michaels of Poison
Seether
Local H
Skid Row
Alter Bridge
Cardboard Vampyres
Living Colour

Mid-gate Stage

Willy Porter/Indigenous/Particle
Donovan
Los Lobos
Peter Himmelman
Galactic
Gin Blossoms
Yonder Mountain String Band
Donna the Buffalo
Cowboy Mouth
Rey Ruiz
Femi Kuti

Potawatomi Classic Rock Stage

Doobie Brothers
Survivor
David Lee Roth
Steve Winwood
John Waite
Styx
Eddie Money
Night Ranger
Whitesnake
Dickey Betts
Southside Johnny

U.S. Cellular Connection

The Neville Brothers
Phantom Planet
Talib Kweli
Gavin DeGraw
Story of the Year
Coheed & Cambria
Umphrey's McGee
Dilated Peoples
Ingram Hill/Marc Broussard
Shelby Lynne/Mindy Smith
Pete Yorn

2006 *June 29-July 9*

Marcus Amphitheater

Tom Petty & the Heartbreakers/Pearl Jam (two nights)
Paul Simon
Nine Inch Nails/Bauhaus/Peaches
Mary J. Blige/Ne-Yo
Kenny Chesney/Jake Owen
Nickelback/Hoobastank/Three Days Grace/Hinder
String Cheese Incident/Bob Weir & Ratdog/Keller Williams
Steely Dan/Michael McDonald
Alan Jackson/Carrie Underwood
Goo Goo Dolls/Counting Crows/Augustana

Local R&B singer Cincere performed at the U.S. Cellular Connection Stage on July 7, 2005.

JOURNAL SENTINEL

Miller Lite Oasis

BoDeans
Los Lonely Boys
David Lee Roth
Kings of Leon
Phil Vassar
Psychedelic Furs
Wilco
The Freddy Jones Band
Train
Guster
Poi Dog Pondering

Briggs & Stratton Big Backyard

Elvis Costello & the Imposters featuring Allen Toussaint
John Kay & Steppenwolf
The Go-Go's
Josh Turner
Alice Cooper
moe.
Flogging Molly
Anthony Hamilton
Cheap Trick
Pink
The Love Monkeys

Harley-Davidson Roadhouse

Common
Lynyrd Skynyrd
Hank Williams Jr.
Dierks Bentley
Rusted Root
Bowling for Soup
Medeski, Martin & Wood
Mixmaster Mike/Digital Underground
Chris Brown
Victor Manuelle
Aqualung

Mountain Dew Rock Stage

Blue Oyster Cult
Everclear
The Gufs
Joan Jett & the Blackhearts
Metal Men
Candlebox
Trapt
Robin Trower
P.O.D.
Seether
Jackyl

**Back cover: The
BoDeans — with
guitarist Kurt Neumann
— originally from
Waukesha, closed
Summerfest 2000
in the Marcus
Amphitheater.**

JOURNAL SENTINEL

**Comedian Lewis
Black cruised the
Summerfest grounds
for fun on July
5, 2005, and got
his picture taken
with Dan Ross of
Tucson, Ariz. Black
had performed the
previous day.**

Potawatomi Casino Stage and Pavilion

Marcia Ball
Cowboy Mouth/Amadou & Miriam
Susan Tedeschi
King Solomon/Fred Hammond
Lewis Black
Elvin Bishop
Mickey Hart & Friends
Floetry
The Big Wu
The Click Five
Buckwheat Zydeco

M&I Bank Classic Rock Stage

REO Speedwagon
Dave Mason
Temptations Review with Dennis Edwards
Ray Davies
Firehouse
Creedence Clearwater Revisited
Foreigner
The Outlaws
Styx
Toto
The Bangles

U.S. Cellular Connection Stage

Keane
Blue October
The All-American Rejects
The Tragically Hip/Soul Asylum
My Morning Jacket
Ryan Cabrera
Mike Doughty's Band
The Fray
Yellowcard
Panic! at the Disco
Jack's Mannequin

MILWAUKEE WORLD FESTIVAL INC